Depart

Switzerland

Jacques Casanova de Seingalt

[ZHINGOORA BOOKS]

DEPART SWITZERLAND

CHAPTER I

The Door—Keeper's Daughters—The Horoscopes—Mdlle. Roman

The idea of the sorry plight in which I had left the Marquis de Prie, his mistress, and perhaps all the company, who had undoubtedly coveted the contents of my cash-box, amused me till I reached Chamberi, where I only stopped to change horses. When I reached Grenoble, where I intended to stay a week, I did not find my lodging to my liking, and went in my carriage to the post-office, where I found several letters, amongst others, one from Madame d'Urfe, enclosing a letter of introduction to an officer named Valenglard, who, she told me, was a learned man, and would present me at all the best houses in the town.

I called on this officer and received a cordial welcome. After reading Madame d'Urfe's letter he said he was ready to be useful to me in anything I pleased.

He was an amiable, middle aged man, and fifteen years before had been Madame d'Urfe's friend, and in a much more intimate degree the friend of her daughter, the Princess de Toudeville. I told him that I was uncomfortable at the inn, and that the first service I would ask of him would be to procure me a comfortable lodging. He rubbed his head, and said,—

"I think I can get you rooms in a beautiful house, but it is outside the town walls. The door-keeper is an excellent cook, and for the sake of doing your cooking I am sure he will lodge you for nothing."

"I don't wish that," said I.

"Don't be afraid," said the baron, "he will make it up by means of his dishes; and besides, the house is for sale and costs him nothing. Come and see it."

I took a suite of three rooms and ordered supper for two, warning the man that I was dainty, liked good things, and did not care for the cost. I also begged M. de Valenglard to sup with me. The doorkeeper said that if I was not pleased with his cooking I had only to say so, and in that case I should have nothing to pay. I sent for my carriage, and felt that I had established myself in my new abode. On the ground floor I saw three charming girls and the door-keeper's wife, who all bowed profoundly. M. de Valenglard took me to a concert with the idea of introducing me to everybody, but I begged him not to do so, as I wished to see the ladies before deciding which of them I should like to know.

The company was a numerous one, especially where women were concerned, but the only one to attract my attention was a pretty and modest-looking brunette, whose fine figure was dressed with great simplicity. Her charming eyes, after having thrown one glance in my direction, obstinately refused to look at me again. My vanity made me conclude at once that she behaved thus only to increase my desire of knowing her, and to give me plenty of time to examine her side-face and her figure, the proportions of which were not concealed by her simple attire. Success begets assurance, and the wish is father to the thought. I cast a hungry gaze on this young lady without more ado, just as if all the women in Europe were only a seraglio kept for my pleasures. I told the baron I should like to know her.

"She is a good girl," said he, "who sees no company, and is quite poor."

"Those are three reasons which make me the more anxious to know her."

"You will really find nothing to do in that quarter."

"Very good."

"There is her aunt, I will introduce you to her as we leave the concert-room."

After doing me this service, he came to sup with me. The door-keeper and cook struck me as being very like Lebel. He made his two pretty daughters wait on me, and I saw that Valenglard was delighted at having lodged me to my satisfaction, but he grumbled when he saw fifteen dishes.

"He is making a fool of you and me," he said.

"On the contrary, he has guessed my tastes. Don't you think everything was very good?"

"I don't deny it, but . . . . "

"Don't be afraid; I love spending my money."

"I beg your pardon, I only want you to be pleased."

We had exquisite wines, and at dessert some ratafia superior to the Turkish 'visnat' I had tasted seventeen years before at Yussuf Ali's.

When my landlord came up at the end of supper, I told him that he   ought to be Louis XV.'s head cook.

"Go on as you have begun, and do better if you can; but let me have your bill every morning."

"You are quite right; with such an arrangement one can tell how one is getting on."

"I should like you always to give me ices, and you must let me have two more lights. But, unless I am mistaken, those are candles that I see. I am a Venetian, and accustomed to wax lights."

"That is your servant's fault, sir."

"How is that?"

"Because, after eating a good supper, he went to bed, saying he was ill.
Thus I heard nothing as to how you liked things done."

"Very good, you shall learn from my own lips."

"He asked my wife to make chocolate for you tomorrow morning; he gave her the chocolate, I will make it myself."

When he had left the room M. de Valenglard said, in a manner that was at the same time pleased and surprised, that Madame d'Urfe had been apparently joking in telling him to spare me all expense.

"It's her goodness of heart. I am obliged to her all the same. She is an excellent woman."

We stayed at table till eleven o'clock, discussing in numerable pleasant topics, and animating our talk with that choice liqueur made at Grenoble, of which we drank a bottle. It is composed of the juice of cherries, brandy, sugar, and cinnamon, and cannot be surpassed, I am sure, by the nectar of Olympus.

I sent home the baron in my carriage, after thanking him for his services, and begging him to be my companion early and late while I stayed at Grenoble—a re quest which he granted excepting for those days on which he was on duty. At supper I had given him my bill of exchange on Zappata, which I endorsed with the name de Seingalt, which Madame d'Urfe had given me. He discounted it for me next day. A banker brought me four hundred louis and I had thirteen hundred in my cash-box. I always had a dread of penuriousness, and I delighted myself at the thought that M. de Valenglard would write and tell Madame d'Urfe, who was always preaching economy to me, what he had seen. I escorted my guest to the carriage, and I was agreeably surprised when I got back to find the doorkeeper's two charming daughters.

Le Duc had not waited for me to tell him to find some pretext for not serving me. He knew my tastes, and that when there were pretty girls in a house, the less I saw of him the better I was pleased.

The frank eagerness of the two girls to wait on me, their utter freedom from suspicion or coquetry, made me determine that I would shew myself deserving of their trust. They took off my shoes and stockings, did my hair and put on my night-gown with perfect propriety on both sides. When I was in bed I wished them a goodnight, and told them to shut the door and bring me my chocolate at eight o'clock next morning.

I could not help confessing that I was perfectly happy as I reflected over my present condition. I enjoyed perfect health, I was in the prime of life, I had no calls on me, I was thoroughly independent, I had a rich store of experience, plenty of money, plenty of luck, and I was a favourite with women. The pains and troubles I had gone through had been followed by so many days of happiness that I felt disposed to bless my destiny. Full of these agreeable thoughts I fell asleep, and all the night my dreams were of happiness and of the pretty brunette who had played with me at the concert.

I woke with thoughts of her, and feeling sure that we should become acquainted I felt curious to know what success I should have with her. She was discreet and poor; and as I was discreet in my own way she ought not to despise my friendship.

At eight o'clock, one of the door-keeper's daughters brought me my chocolate, and told me that Le Duc had got the fever.

"You must take care of the poor fellow."

"My cousin has just taken him some broth."

"What is your name?"

"My name is Rose, and my sister is Manon."

Just then Manon came in with my shirt, on which she had put fresh lace. I thanked her, and she said with a blush that she did her father's hair very well.

"I am delighted to hear it, and I shall be very pleased if you will be kind enough to do the same offices for me till my servant recovers."

"With pleasure, sir."

"And I," said Rose, laughing, "will shave you."

"I should like to see how you do it; get the water."

I rose hastily, while Manon was preparing to do my hair. Rose returned and shaved me admirably. As soon as she had washed off the lather, I said,

"You must give me a kiss," presenting my cheek to her. She pretended not to understand.

"I shall be vexed," said I, gravely but pleasantly, "if you refuse to kiss me."

She begged to be excused, saying with a little smile, that it was not customary to do so at Grenoble.

"Well, if you won't kiss me, you shan't shave me."

The father came in at that point, bringing his bill.

"Your daughter has just shaved me admirably," said I, "and she refuses to kiss me, because it is not the custom at Grenoble."

"You little silly," said he, "it is the custom in Paris. You kiss me fast enough after you have shaved me, why should you be less polite to this gentleman?"

She then kissed me with an air of submission to the paternal decree which made Manon laugh.

"Ah!" said the father, "your turn will come when you have finished doing the gentleman's hair."

He was a cunning fellow, who knew the best way to prevent me cheapening him, but there was no need, as I thought his charges reasonable, and as I paid him in full he went off in great glee.

Manon did my hair as well as my dear Dubois, and kissed me when she had done without making as many difficulties as Rose. I thought I should get on well with both of them. They went downstairs when the banker was announced.

He was quite a young man, and after he had counted me out four hundred
Louis, he observed that I must be very comfortable.

"Certainly," said I, "the two sisters are delightful."

"Their cousin is better. They are too discreet."

"I suppose they are well off."

"The father has two thousand francs a year. They will be able to marry well-to-do tradesmen."

I was curious to see the cousin who was said to be prettier than the sisters, and as soon as the banker had gone I went downstairs to satisfy my curiosity. I met the father and asked him which was Le Duc's room, and thereon I went to see my fine fellow. I found him sitting up in a comfortable bed with a rubicund face which did not look as if he were dangerously ill.

"What is the matter with you?

"Nothing, sir. I am having a fine time of it. Yesterday I thought I would be ill."

"What made you think that?"

"The sight of the three Graces here, who are made of better stuff than your handsome housekeeper, who would not let me kiss her. They are making me wait too long for my broth, however. I shall have to speak severely about it."

"Le Duc, you are a rascal."

"Do you want me to get well?"

"I want you to put a stop to this farce, as I don't like it." Just then the door opened, and the cousin came in with the broth. I thought her ravishing, and I noticed that in waiting on Le Duc she had an imperious little air which well became her.

11

"I shall dine in bed," said my Spaniard.

"You shall be attended to," said the pretty girl, and she went out.

"She puts on big airs," said Le Duc, "but that does not impose on me.
Don't you think she is very pretty?"

"I think you are very impudent. You ape your betters, and I don't approve of it. Get up. You must wait on me at table, and afterwards you will eat your dinner by yourself, and try to get yourself respected as an honest man always is, whatever his condition, so long as he does not forget himself. You must not stay any longer in this room, the doorkeeper will give you another."

I went out, and on meeting the fair cousin I told her that I was jealous of the honour which she had done my man, and that I begged her to wait on him no longer.

"Oh, I am very glad!"

The door-keeper came up, and I gave him my orders, and went back to my room to write.

Before dinner the baron came and told me that he had just come from the lady to whom he had introduced me. She was the wife of a barrister named Morin, and aunt to the young lady who had so interested me.

"I have been talking of you," said the baron, "and of the impression her niece made on you. She promised to send for her, and to keep her at the house all day."

After a dinner as good as the supper of the night before, though different from it in its details, and appetising enough to awaken the dead, we went to see Madame Morin, who received us with the easy grace of a Parisian lady. She introduced me to seven children, of whom she was the mother. Her eldest daughter, an ordinary-looking girl, was twelve years old, but I should have taken her to be fourteen, and said so. To convince me of her age the mother brought a book in which the year, the month, the day, the hour, and even the minute of her birth were entered. I was astonished at such minute accuracy, and asked if she had had a horoscope drawn.

"No," said she, "I have never found anybody to do it."

"It is never too late," I replied, "and without doubt God has willed that this pleasure should be reserved for me."

At this moment M. Morin came in, his wife introduced me, and after the customary compliments had passed, she returned to the subject of the horoscope. The barrister sensibly observed that if judicial astrology was not wholly false, it was, nevertheless, a suspected science; that he had been so foolish as once to devote a considerable portion of his time to it, but that on recognizing the inability of man to deal with the future he had abandoned astrology, contenting himself with the veritable truths of astronomy. I saw with pleasure that I had to deal with a man of sense and education, but Valenglard, who was a believer in astrology, began an argument with him on the subject. During their discussion I quietly copied out on my tablets the date of Mdlle. Morin's birth. But M. Morin saw what I was about, and shook his head at me, with a smile. I understood what he meant, but I did not allow that to disconcert me, as I had made up my mind fully five minutes ago that I would play the astrologer on this occasion.

At last the fair niece arrived. Her aunt introduced me to her as Mdlle. Roman Coupier, her sister's daughter; and then, turning to her, she informed her how ardently I had been longing to know her since I had seen her at the concert.

She was then seventeen. Her satin skin by its dazzling whiteness displayed to greater advantage her magnificent black hair. Her features were perfectly regular, and her complexion had a slight tinge of red; her fine eyes were at once sweet and sparkling, her eyebrows were well arched, her mouth small, her teeth regular and as white as pearls, and her lips, of an exquisite rosy hue, afforded a seat to the deities of grace and modesty.

After some moments' conversation, M. Morin was obliged to go out on business, and a game of quadrille was proposed, at which I was greatly pitied for having lost a louis. I thought Mdlle. Roman discreet, judicious, pleasant without being brilliant, and, still better, without any pretensions. She was high-spirited, even-tempered, and had a natural art which did not allow her to seem to understand too flattering a compliment, or a joke which passed in any way the bounds of propriety. She was neatly dressed, but had no ornaments, and nothing which shewed wealth; neither ear-rings, rings, nor a watch. One might have said that her beauty was her only adornment, the only ornament she wore being a small gold cross hanging from her necklace of black ribbon. Her breast was well shaped and not too large. Fashion and custom made her shew half of it as innocently as she shewed her plump white hand, or her cheeks, whereon the lily and the rose were wedded. I looked at her features to see if I might hope at all; but I was completely puzzled, and could come to no conclusion. She gave no sign which made me hope, but on the other hand she did nothing to make me despair. She was so natural and so reserved that my sagacity was completely at fault. Nevertheless, a liberty which I took at supper gave me a gleam of hope. Her napkin fell down, and in returning it to her I pressed her thigh amorously, and could not detect the slightest displeasure on her features. Content with so much I begged everybody to come to dinner with me next day, telling Madame Morin that I should not be going out, and that I was therefore delighted to put my carriage at her service.

When I had taken Valenglard home, I went to my lodging building castles in Spain as to the conquest of Mdlle. Roman.

I warned my landlord that we should be six at dinner and supper the following day, and then I went to bed. As Le Duc was undressing me he said,

"Sir, you are punishing me, but what makes me sorry you are punishing yourself in depriving yourself of the services of those pretty girls."

"You are a rogue."

"I know it, but I serve you with all my heart, and I love your pleasure as well as my own."

"You plead well for yourself; I am afraid I have spoilt you."

"Shall I do your hair to-morrow?"

"No; you may go out every day till dinner-time."

"I shall be certain to catch it."

"Then I shall send you to the hospital."

"That is a fine prospect, 'por Dios'."

He was impudent, sly, profligate, and a rascally fellow; but also obedient, devoted, discreet, and faithful, and his good qualities made me overlook his defects.

Next morning, when Rose brought my chocolate, she told me with a laugh that my man had sent for a carriage, and after dressing himself in the height of fashion he had gone off with his sword at his side, to pay calls, as he said.

"We laughed at him."

"You were quite right, my dear Rose."

As I spoke, Manon came in under some pretext or other. I saw that the two sisters had an understanding never to be alone with me; I was displeased, but pretended not to notice anything. I got up, and I had scarcely put on my dressing-gown when the cousin came in with a packet under her arm.

"I am delighted to see you, and above all to look at your smiling face, for I thought you much too serious yesterday."

"That's because M. le Duc is a greater gentleman than you are; I should not have presumed to laugh in his presence; but I had my reward in seeing him start off this morning in his gilded coach."

"Did he see you laughing at him?"

"Yes, unless he is blind."

"He will be vexed."

"All the better."

"You are really very charming. What have you got in that parcel?"

"Some goods of our own manufacture. Look; they are embroidered gloves."

"They are beautiful; the embroidery is exquisitely done. How much for the lot?"

"Are you a good hand at a bargain."

"Certainly."

"Then we must take that into account."

After some whisperings together the cousin took a pen, put down the numbers of gloves, added up and said,

"The lot will cost you two hundred and ten francs."

"There are nine louis; give me six francs change."

"But you told us you would make a bargain."

"You were wrong to believe it."

She blushed and gave me the six francs. Rose and Manon shaved me and did my hair, giving me a kiss with the best grace imaginable; and when I offered my cheek to the cousin she kissed me on the mouth in a manner that told me she would be wholly mine on the first opportunity.

"Shall we have the pleasure of waiting on you at the table?" said Rose.

"I wish you would."

"But we should like to know who is coming to dinner first; as if it is officers from the garrison we dare not come; they make so free."

"My guests are Madame Morin, her husband, and her niece."

"Very good."

The cousin said, "Mdlle. Roman is the prettiest and the best girl in Grenoble; but she will find some difficulty in marrying as she has no money."

"She may meet some rich man who will think her goodness and her beauty worth a million of money."

"There are not many men of that kind."

"No; but there are a few."

Manon and the cousin went out, and I was left alone with Rose, who stayed to dress me. I attacked her, but she defended herself so resolutely that I desisted, and promised it should not occur again. When she had finished I gave her a louis, thanked her, and sent her away.

As soon as I was alone I locked the door, and proceeded to concoct the horoscope I had promised to Madame Morin. I found it an easy task to fill eight pages with learned folly; and I confined myself chiefly to declaring the events which had already happened to the native. I had deftly extracted some items of information in the course of conversation, and filling up the rest according to the laws of probability and dressing up the whole in astrological diction, I was pronounced to be a seer, and no doubts were cast on my skill. I did not indeed run much risk, for everything hung from an if, and in the judicious employment of ifs lies the secret of all astrology.

I carefully re-read the document, and thought it admirable. I felt in the vein, and the use of the cabala had made me an expert in this sort of thing.

Just after noon all my guests arrived, and at one we sat down to table. I have never seen a more sumptuous or more delicate repast. I saw that the cook was an artist more in need of restraint than encouragement. Madame Morin was very polite to the three girls, whom she knew well, and Le Duc stood behind her chair all the time, looking after her wants, and dressed as richly as the king's chamberlain. When we had nearly finished dinner Mdlle. Roman passed a compliment on my three fair waiting-maids, and this giving me occasion to speak of their talents I got up and brought the gloves I had purchased from them. Mdlle. Roman praised the quality of the material and the work. I took the opportunity, and begged leave of the aunt to give her and her niece a dozen pair apiece. I obtained this favour, and I then gave Madame Morin the horoscope. Her husband read it, and though an unbeliever he was forced to admire, as all the deductions were taken naturally from the position of the heavenly bodies at the instant of his daughter's birth. We spent a couple of hours in talking about astrology, and the same time in playing at quadrille, and then we took a walk in the garden, where I was politely left to enjoy the society of the fair Roman.

Our dialogue, or rather my monologue, turned solely on the profound impression she had made on me, on the passion she had inspired, on her beauty, her goodness, the purity of my intentions, and on my need of love, lest I should go down to the grave the most hapless of men.

"Sir," said she, at last, "if my destiny points to marriage I do not deny that I should be happy to find a husband like you."

I was emboldened by this frank declaration, and seizing her hand I covered it with fiery kisses, saying passionately that I hoped she would not let me languish long. She turned her head to look for her aunt. It was getting dark, and she seemed to be afraid of something happening to her. She drew me gently with her, and on rejoining the other guests we returned to the dining-room, where I made a small bank at faro for their amusement. Madame Morin gave her daughter and niece, whose pockets were empty, some money, and Valenglard directed their play so well that when we left off to go to supper I had the pleasure of seeing that each of the three ladies had won two or three louis.

We sat at table till midnight. A cold wind from the Alps stopped my plan of proposing a short turn in the garden. Madame Morin overwhelmed me with thanks for my entertainment, and I gave each of my lady-visitors a respectful kiss.

I heard singing in the kitchen, and on going in I found Le Duc in a high state of excitement and very drunk. As soon as he saw me he tried to rise, but he lost his centre of gravity, and fell right under the kitchen table. He was carried away to bed.

I thought this accident favourable to my desire of amusing myself, and I might have succeeded if the three Graces had not all been there. Love only laughs when two are present, and thus it is that the ancient mythology tells no story of the loves of the Graces, who were always together. I had not yet found an opportunity of getting my three maids one after the other, and I dared not risk a general attack, which might have lost me the confidence of each one. Rose, I saw, was openly jealous of her cousin, as she kept a keen look-out after her movements. I was not sorry, for jealousy leads to anger, and anger goes a long way. When I was in bed I sent them away with a modest good night.

Next morning, Rose came in by herself to ask me for a cake of chocolate, for, as she said, Le Duc was now ill in real earnest. She brought me the box, and I gave her the chocolate, and in doing so I took her hand and shewed her how well I loved her. She was offended, drew back her hand sharply, and left the room. A moment after Manon came in under the pretext of shewing me a piece of lace I had torn away in my attempts of the day before, and of asking me if she should mend it. I took her hand to kiss it, but she did not give me time, presenting her lips, burning with desire. I took her hand again, and it was just on the spot when the cousin came in. Manon held the piece of lace, and seemed to be waiting for my answer. I told her absently that I should be obliged if she would mend it when she had time, and with this she went out.

I was troubled by this succession of disasters, and thought that the cousin would not play me false from the earnest of her affection which she had given me the day before in that ardent kiss of hers. I begged her to give me my handkerchief, and gently drew her hand towards me. Her mouth fastened to mine, and her hand, which she left to my pleasure with all the gentleness of a lamb, was already in motion when Rose came in with my chocolate. We regained our composure in a moment, but I was furious at heart. I scowled at Rose, and I had a right to do so after the manner in which she had repulsed me a quarter of an hour before. Though the chocolate was excellent, I pronounced it badly made. I chid her for her awkwardness in waiting on me, and repulsed her at every step. When I got up I would not let her shave me; I shaved myself, which seemed to humiliate her, and then

Manon did my hair. Rose and the cousin then went out, as if to make common cause together, but it was easy to see that Rose was less angry with her sister than her cousin.

As Manon was finishing my toilette, M. de Valenglard came in. As soon as we were alone, the officer, who was a man of honour and of much sense, in spite of his belief in astrology and the occult sciences, said that he thought me looking rather melancholy, and that if my sadness had any connection with the fair Roman, he warned me to think no more of her, unless I had resolved to ask her hand in marriage. I replied that to put an end to all difficulties I had decided on leaving Grenoble in a few days. We dined together and we then called on Madame Morin, with whom we found her fair niece.

Madame Morin gave me a flattering welcome, and Mdlle. Roman received me so graciously that I was emboldened to kiss her and place her on my knee. The aunt laughed, the niece blushed, and then slipping into my hand a little piece of paper made her escape. I read on the paper the year, day, Hour, and minute of her birth, and guessed what she meant. She meant, I thought, that I could do nothing with her before I had drawn up her horoscope. My resolve was soon taken to profit by this circumstance, and I told her that I would tell her whether I could oblige her or not next day, if she would come to a ball I was giving. She looked at her aunt and my invitation was accepted.

Just then the servant announced "The Russian Gentleman." I saw a well-made man of about my own age, slightly marked with the small-pox, and dressed as a traveller. He accosted Madame Morin with easy grace, was welcomed heartily by her, spoke well, scarcely gave me a glance, and did not say a word to the nieces. In the evening M. Morin came in, and the Russian gave him a small phial full of a white liquid, and then made as if he would go, but he was kept to supper.

At table the conversation ran on this marvellous liquid of his. M. Morin told me that he had cured a young man of a bruise from a billiard ball in five minutes, by only rubbing it with the liquid. He said modestly that it was a trifling thing of his own invention, and he talked a good deal about chemistry to Valenglard. As my attention was taken up by the fair Mdlle. Roman I could not take part in their conversation; my hope of succeeding with her on the following day absorbed all my thoughts. As I was going away with Valenglard he told me that nobody knew who the Russian was, and that he was nevertheless received everywhere.

"Has he a carriage and servants?"

"He has nothing, no servants and no money."

"Where did he come from?"

"From the skies."

"A fair abode, certainly; how long has he been here?"

"For the last fortnight. He visits, but asks for nothing."

"How does he live?"

"On credit at the inn; he is supposed to be waiting for his carriage and servants."

"He is probably a vagabond."

"He does not look like one, as you saw for yourself, and his diamonds contradict that hypothesis."

"Yes, if they are not imitation stones, for it seems to me that if they were real he would sell them."

When I got home Rose came by herself to attend on me, but she continued to sulk. I tried to rouse her up, but as I had no success I ordered her to go and tell her father that I was going to give a ball next day in the room by the garden, and that supper was to be laid for twenty.

When the door-keeper came to take my orders the following morning, I told him that I should like his girls to dance if he didn't mind. At this Rose condescended to smile, and I thought it a good omen. Just as she went out with her father, Manon came in under the pretext of asking me what lace I would wear for the day. I found her as gentle as a lamb and as loving as a dove. The affair was happily consummated, but we had a narrow escape of being caught by Rose, who came in with Le Duc and begged me to let him dance, promising that he would behave himself properly. I was glad that everybody should enjoy themselves and consented, telling him to thank Rose, who had got him this favour.

I had a note from Madame Morin, asking me if she might bring with her to the ball two ladies of her acquaintance and their daughters. I replied that I should be delighted for her to invite not only as many ladies but as many gentlemen as she pleased, as I had ordered supper for twenty people. She came to dinner with her niece and Valenglard, her daughter being busy dressing and her husband being engaged till the evening. She assured me that I should have plenty of guests.

The fair Mdlle. Roman wore the same dress, but her beauty unadorned was dazzling. Standing by me she asked if I had thought about her horoscope. I took her hand, made her sit on my knee, and promised that she should have it on the morrow. I held her thus, pressing her charming breasts with my left hand, and imprinting fiery kisses on her lips, which she only opened to beg me to calm myself. She was more astonished than afraid to see me trembling, and though she defended herself successfully she did not lose countenance for a moment, and in spite of my ardent gaze she did not turn her face away. I calmed myself with an effort, and her eyes expressed the satisfaction of one who has vanquished a generous enemy by the force of reason. By my silence I praised the virtue of this celestial being, in whose destiny I only had a part by one of those caprices of chance which philosophy seeks to explain in vain.

Madame Morin came up to me, and asked me to explain some points in her daughter's horoscope. She then told me that if I wanted to have four beauties at my ball she had only to write a couple of notes.

"I shall only see one beauty," said I, looking at her niece.

"God alone knows," said Valenglard, "what people will say in Grenoble!"

"They will say it is your wedding ball," said Madame Morin to her niece.

"Yes, and they will doubtless talk of my magnificent dress, my lace, and my diamonds," said the niece, pleasantly.

"They will talk of your beauty, your wit, and your goodness," I replied, passionately, "goodness which will make your husband a happy man."

There was a silence, because they all thought I was alluding to myself. I was doing nothing of the sort. I should have been glad to give five hundred louis for her, but I did not see how the contract was to be drawn up, and I was not going to throw my money away.

We went to my bedroom, and while Mdlle. Roman was amusing herself with looking at the jewelry on my toilette-table, her aunt and Valenglard examined the books on the table by my bedside. I saw Madame Morin going to the window and looking closely at something she held in her hand. I remembered I had left out the portrait of the fair nun. I ran to her and begged her to give me the indecent picture I had so foolishly left about.

"I don't mind the indecency of it," she said, "but what strikes me is the exact likeness."

I understood everything, and I shuddered at the carelessness of which I had been guilty.

"Madam," I said, "that is the portrait of a Venetian, lady, of whom I was very found."

"I daresay, but it's very curious. These two M's, these cast-off robes sacrificed to love, everything makes my surprise greater."

"She is a nun and named M—— M——."

"And a Welsh niece of mine at Camberi is also named M—— M——, and belongs to the same order. Nay, more, she has been at Aix, whence you have come, to get cured of an illness."

"And this portrait is like her?"

"As one drop of water is like another."

"If you go to Chamberi call on her and say you come from me; you will be welcome and you will be as much surprised as I am."

"I will do so, after I have been in Italy. However, I will not shew her this portrait, which would scandalize her; I will put it away carefully."

"I beg you not to shew it to anyone."

"You may rely on me."

I was in an ecstasy at having put her off so effectually.

At eight o'clock all my guests arrived, and I saw before me all the fairest ladies and the noblest gentlemen of Grenoble. The only thing which vexed me was the compliments they lavished on me, as is customary in the provinces.

I opened the ball with the lady pointed out to me by M. Valenglard, and then I danced with all the ladies in succession; but my partner in all the square dances was the fair Mdlle. Roman, who shone from her simplicity—at least, in my eyes.

After a quadrille, in which I had exerted myself a good deal, I felt hot and went up to my room to put on a lighter suit, and as I was doing so, in came the fair cousin, who asked me if I required anything.

"Yes, you, dearest," I replied, going up to her and taking her in my arms. "Did anyone see you coming in here?"

"No, I came from upstairs, and my cousins are in the dancing-room."

"That is capital. You are fair as Love himself, and this is an excellent opportunity for skewing you how much I love you."

"Good heavens! What are you doing? Let me go, somebody might come   in.
Well, put out the light!"

I put it out, shut the door, and, my head full of Mdlle. Roman, the cousin found me as ardent as I should have been with that delightful person. I confess, too, that the door-keeper's niece was well worthy of being loved on her own merits. I found her perfect, perhaps better than Mdlle. Roman, a novice, would have been. In spite of my ardour her passion was soon appeased, and she begged me to let her go, and I did so; but it was quite time. I wanted to begin over again, but she was afraid that our absence would be noticed by her two Argus-eyed cousins, so she kissed me and left the room.

I went back to the ball-room, and we danced on till the king of door-keepers came to tell us supper was ready.

A collation composed of the luxuries which the season and the country afforded covered the table; but what pleased the ladies most was the number and artistic arrangement of the wax lights.

I sat down at a small table with a few of my guests, and I received the most pressing invitations to spend the autumn in their town. I am sure that if I had accepted I should have been treated like a prince, for the nobility of Grenoble bear the highest character for hospitality. I told them that if it had been possible I should have had the greatest pleasure in accepting their invitation, and in that case I should have been delighted to have made the acquaintance of the family of an illustrious gentleman, a friend of my father's.

"What name is it?" they asked me, altogether.

"Bouchenu de Valbonnais."

"He was my uncle. Ah! sir, you must come and stay with us. You danced with my daughter. What was your father's name?"

This story, which I invented, and uttered as I was wont, on the spur of the moment, turned me into a sort of wonder in the eyes of the worthy people.

After we had laughed, jested, drank, and eaten, we rose from the table and began to dance anew.

Seeing Madame Morin, her niece, and Valenglard going into the garden, I followed them, and as we walked in the moonlight I led the fair Mdlle. Roman through a covered alley; but all my fine speeches were in vain; I could do nothing. I held her between my arms, I covered her with burning kisses, but not one did she return to me, and her hands offered a successful resistance to my hardy attempts. By a sudden effort, however, I at last attained the porch of the temple of love, and held her in such a way that further resistance would have been of no avail; but she stopped me short by saying in a voice which no man of feeling could have resisted,—

"Be my friend, sir, and not my enemy and the cause of my ruin."

I knelt before her, and taking her hand begged her pardon, swearing not to renew my attempts. I then rose and asked her to kiss me as a pledge of her forgiveness. We rejoined her aunt, and returned to the ball-room, but with all my endeavours I could not regain my calm.

I sat down in a corner of the room, and I asked Rose, who passed by me, to get me a glass of lemonade. When she brought it she gently chid me for not having danced with her, her sister, or her cousin.

"It will give people but a poor opinion of our merits."

"I am tired," said I, "but if you will promise to be kind I will dance a minuet with you."

"What do want me to do?" said she.

"Go into my bedroom and wait for me there in the dark when you see your sister and your cousin busy dancing."

"And you will only dance with me."

"I swear!"

"Then you will find me in your room."

I found her passionate, and I had full satisfaction. To keep my word with her I waited for the closing minuet, for having danced with Rose I felt obliged in common decency to dance with the other two, especially as I owed them the same debt.

At day-break the ladies began to vanish, and as I put the Morins into my carriage I told them that I could not have the pleasure of seeing them again that day, but that if they would come and spend the whole of the day after with me I would have the horoscope ready.

I went to the kitchen to thank the worthy door-keeper for having made me cut such a gallant figure, and I found the three nymphs there, filling their pockets with sweetmeats. He told them, laughing, that as the master was there they might rob him with a clear conscience, and I bade them take as much as they would. I informed the door-keeper that I should not dine till six, and I then went to bed.

I awoke at noon, and feeling myself well rested I set to work at the horoscope, and I resolved to tell the fair Mdlle. Roman that fortune awaited her at Paris, where she would become her master's mistress, but that the monarch must see her before she had attained her eighteenth year, as at that time her destiny would take a different turn. To give my prophecy authority, I told her some curious circumstances which had hitherto happened to her, and which I had learnt now and again from herself or Madame Morin without pretending to heed what they said.

With an Ephemeris and another astrological book, I made out and copied in six hours Mdlle. Roman's horoscope, and I had so well arranged it that it struck Valenglard and even M. Morin with astonishment, and made the two ladies quite enthusiastic.

My horoscope must only be known to the young lady and her family, who would no doubt keep the secret well. After I had put the finishing touches to it, read it, and read it again, I felt certain that I had made a masterpiece, and I then dined in bed with my three nymphs. I was polite and affectionate to them all, and we were all happy together, but I was the happiest. M. de Valenglard came to see me early the next day, and informed me that nobody suspected me of being in love with Mdlle. Roman, but that I was thought to be amorous of my landlord's girls.

"Well, let them think so," said I; "they are worthy of love, though not to be named in the same breath with one past compare, but who leaves me no hope."

"Let me tell Madame d'Urfe all about it."

"Certainly; I shall be delighted."

M. and Madame Morin and their niece came at noon, and we spent the hour before dinner in reading the horoscope. It would be impossible to describe the four distinct sorts of surprise which I saw before me. The interesting Mdlle. Roman looked very grave, and, not knowing whether she had a will of her own, listened to what was said in silence. M. Morin looked at me now and again, and seeing that I kept a serious countenance did not dare to laugh. Valenglard shewed fanatic belief in astrology in every feature. Madame Morin seemed struck as by a miracle, and, far from thinking the fact prophesied too improbable, remarked that her niece was much more worthy of becoming her sovereign's wife or mistress than the bigoted Maintenon had been.

"She would never have done anything," said Madame Morin, "if she had not left America and come to France; and if my niece does not go to Paris nobody can say that the horoscope has prophesied falsely. We should therefore—go to Paris, but how is it to be done? I don't see my way to it. The prediction of the birth of a son has something divine and entrancing about it. I don't wish to seem prejudiced, but my niece has certainly more qualifications for gaining the king's affection than the Maintenon had: my niece is a good girl and young, while the Maintenon was no longer as young as she had been, and had led a strange life before she became a devotee. But we shall never accomplish this journey to Paris."

"Nay," said Valenglard, in a serious tone, which struck me as supremely ridiculous, "she must go; her fate must be fulfilled."

The fair Mdlle. Roman seemed all amazed. I let them talk on, and we sat down to dinner.

[The next two paragraphs were misplaced in the original, likely by the typesetter, and have been inserted here where it seems that they belong. D.W.]

I hoped I should be asked to take the diamond to Paris myself, and I felt inclined to grant the request. I flattered myself that they could not do without me, and that I should get what I wanted, if not for love at any rate through gratitude; indeed, who knew what might become of the plan? The monarch would be sure to be caught directly. I had no doubts on that subject, for where is the man in love who does not think that his beloved object will win the hearts of all others? For the moment I felt quite jealous of the king, but, from my thorough knowledge of my own inconstancy, I felt sure that my jealousy would cease when my love had been rewarded, and I was aware that Louis XV. did not altogether hold the opinions of a Turk in such concerns. What gave an almost divine character to the horoscope was the prediction of a son to be born, who would make the happiness of France, and could only come from the royal blood and from a singular vessel of election.

A curious fancy increased my delight, namely, the thought of becoming a famous astrologer in an age when reason and science had so justly demolished astrology. I enjoyed the thought of seeing myself sought out by crowned heads, which are always the more accessible to superstitious notions. I determined I would be particular to whom I gave my advice. Who has not made his castles in Spain? If Mdlle. Roman gave birth to a daughter instead of a son I should be amused, and all would not be lost, for a son might come afterwards.

At first silence reigned, and then the conversation ran on a thousand trifles, as is usual in good society, but by degrees, as I had thought, they returned to the horoscope.

"According to the horoscope," said the aunt, "the king is to fall in love with my niece in her eighteenth year; she is now close on it. What are we to do? Where are we to get the hundred louis necessary? And when she gets to Paris is she to go to the king and say, 'Here I am, your majesty'? And who is going to take her there? I can't."

"My aunt Roman might," said the young lady, blushing up to her eyes at the roar of laughter which none of us could restrain.

"Well," said Madame Morin, "there is Madame Varnier, of the Rue de Richelieu; she is an aunt of yours. She has a good establishment, and knows everybody."

"See," said Valenglard, "how the ways of destiny are made plain. You talk of a hundred louis; twelve will be sufficient to take you to Madame Varnier's. When you get there, leave the rest to your fate, which will surely favour you."

"If you do go to Paris," said I, "say nothing to Madame Roman or Madame
Varnier about the horoscope."

"I will say nothing to anyone about it; but, after all, it is only a happy dream. I shall never see Paris, still less Louis XV."

I arose, and going to my cash-box I took out a roll of a hundred and fifty louis, which I gave to her, saying it was a packet of sweetmeats. It felt rather heavy, and on opening it she found it to contain fifty pieces-of-eight, which she took for medals.

"They are gold," said Valenglard.

"And the goldsmith will give you a hundred and fifty louis for them," added M. Morin.

"I beg you will keep them; you can give me a bill payable at Paris when you become rich."

I knew she would refuse to accept my present, although I should have been delighted if she had kept the money. But I admired her strength of mind in restraining her tears, and that without disturbing for a moment the smile on her face.

We went out to take a turn in the garden. Valenglard and Madame Morin began on the topic of the horoscope anew, and I left them, taking Mdlle. Roman with me.

"I wish you would tell me," said she, when we were out of hearing of the others, "if this horoscope is not all a joke."

"No," I answered, "it is quite serious, but it all depends on an if. If you do not go to Paris the prophecy will never be fulfilled."

"You must think so, certainly, or you would never have offered me those fifty medals."

"Do me the pleasure of accepting them now; nobody will know anything about it."

"No, I cannot, though I am much obliged to you. But why should you want to give me such a large sum?"

"For the pleasure of contributing to your happiness, and in the hope that you will allow me to love you."

"If you really love met why should I oppose your love? You need not buy my consent; and to be happy I do not want to possess the King of France, if you did but know to what my desires are limited."

"Tell me."

"I would fain find a kind husband, rich enough for us not to lack the necessaries of life."

"But how if you did not love him?"

"If he was a good, kind man how could I help loving him?"

"I see that you do not know what love is."

"You are right. I do not know the love that maddens, and I thank God for it."

"Well, I think you are wise; may God preserve you from that love."

"You say, that as soon as the king sees me he will fall in love with me, and to tell you the truth that strikes me as vastly improbable; for though it is quite possible that he may not think me plain, or he might even pronounce me pretty, yet I do not think he will become so madly in love as you say."

"You don't? Let us sit down. You have only got to fancy that the king will take the same liking to you that I have done; that is all."

"But what do you find in me that you will not find in most girls of my age? I certainly may have struck you; but that only proves that I was born to exercise this sway over you, and not at all that I am to rule the king in like manner. Why should I go and look for the king, if you love me yourself?"

"Because I cannot give you the position you deserve."

"I should have thought you had plenty of money."

"Then there's another reason: you are not in love with me."

"I love you as tenderly as if I were your wife. I might then kiss you, though duty now forbids my doing so."

"I am much obliged to you for not being angry with me for being so happy with you!"

"On the contrary, I am delighted to please you."

"Then you will allow me to call on you at an early hour to-morrow, and to take coffee at your bedside."

"Do not dream of such a thing. If I would I could not. I sleep with my aunt, and I always rise at the same time she does. Take away your hand; you promised not to do it again. In God's name, let me alone."

Alas! I had to stop; there was no overcoming her. But what pleased me extremely was that in spite of my amorous persecution she did not lose that smiling calm which so became her. As for myself I looked as if I deserved that pardon for which I pleaded on my knees, and in her eyes I read that she was sorry that she could not grant what I required of her.

I could no longer stay beside her, my senses were too excited by her beauty. I left her and went to my room where I found the kind Manon busying herself on my cuffs, and she gave me the relief I wanted, and when we were both satisfied made her escape. I reflected that I should never obtain more than I had obtained hitherto from young Mdlle. Roman—at least, unless I gave the lie to my horoscope by marrying her, and I decided that I would not take any further steps in the matter. I returned to the garden, and going up to the aunt I begged her to walk with me. In vain I urged the worthy woman to accept a hundred louis for her niece's journey from me. I swore to her by all I held sacred that no one else should ever know of the circumstance. All my eloquence and all my prayers were in vain. She told me that if her niece's destiny only depended on that journey all would be well, for she had thought over a plan which would, with her husband's consent, enable Mdlle. Roman to go to Paris. At the same time she gave me her sincerest thanks, and said that her niece was very fortunate to have pleased me so well.

"She pleased me so well," I replied, "that I have resolved to go away to-morrow to avoid making proposals to you which would bring the great fortune that awaits her to nought. If it were not for that I should have been happy to have asked her hand of you."

"Alas! her happiness would, perhaps, be built on a better foundation.
Explain yourself."

"I dare not wage war with fate."

"But you are not going to-morrow?"

"Excuse me, but I shall call to take leave at two o'clock."

The news of my approaching departure saddened the supper-table. Madame Morin, who, for all I know, may be alive now, was a most kind-hearted woman. At table she announced her resolve that as I had decided on going, and as I should only leave my house to take leave of her, she would not force me to put myself out to such an extent, and ordained that our farewells should be said that evening.

"At least," I said, "I may have the honour of escorting you to your door?"

"That will protract our happiness for some minutes." Valenglard went away on foot, and the fair Mdlle. Roman sat on my knee. I dared to be bold with her, and contrary to expectation she shewed herself so kind that I was half sorry I was going; but the die was cast.

A carriage lying overturned on the road outside an inn made my coachman stop a short while, and this accident which made the poor driver curse overwhelmed me with joy, for in these few moments I obtained all the favours that she could possibly give under the circumstances.

Happiness enjoyed alone is never complete. Mine was not until I assured myself, by looking at my sweetheart's features, that the part she had taken had not been an entirely passive one; and I escorted the ladies to their room. There, without any conceit, I was certain that I saw sadness and love upon that fair creature's face. I could see that she was neither cold nor insensible, and that the obstacles she had put in my way were only suggested by fear and virtue. I gave Madame Morin a farewell kiss, and she was kind enough to tell her niece to give me a similar mark of friendship, which she did in a way that shewed me how completely she had shared my ardour.

I left them, feeling amorous and sorry I had obliged myself to go. On entering my room I found the three nymphs together, which vexed me as I only wanted one. I whispered my wishes to Rose as she curled my hair, but she told me it was impossible for her to slip away as they all slept in one room. I then told them that I was going away the next day, and that if they would pass the night with me I would give them a present of six louis each. They laughed at my proposal and said it couldn't possibly be done. I saw by this they had not made confidantes of one another, as girls mostly do, and I also saw that they were jealous of each other. I wished them a good night, and as soon as I was in bed the god of dreams took me under his care, and made me pass the night with the adorable Mdlle. Roman.

I rang rather late in the morning, and the cousin came in and said that Rose would bring my chocolate, and that M. Charles Ivanoff wanted to speak to me. I guessed that this was the

Russian, but as he had not been introduced to me I thought I might decline to see him.

"Tell him I don't know his name."

Rose went out, and came in again saying he was the gentleman who had had the honour of supping with me at Madame Morin's.

"Tell him to come in."

"Sir," said he, "I want to speak with you in private."

"I cannot order these young ladies to leave my room, sir. Be kind enough to wait for me outside till I have put on my dressing-gown, and then I shall be ready to speak to you."

"If I am troubling you, I will call again to-morrow."

"You would not find me, as I am leaving Grenoble to-day."

"In that case I will wait."

I got up in haste and went out to him.

"Sir," said he, "I must leave this place, and I have not a penny to pay my landlord. I beg of you to come to my aid. I dare not have recourse to anyone else in the town for fear of exposing myself to the insult of a refusal."

"Perhaps I ought to feel myself flattered at the preference you have shewn me, but without wishing to insult you in any way I am afraid I shall be obliged to refuse your request."

"If you knew who I am I am sure you would not refuse me some small help."

"If you think so, tell me who you are; you may count on my silence."

"I am Charles, second son of Ivan, Duke of Courland, who is in exile in Siberia. I made my escape."

"If you go to Genoa you will find yourself beyond the reach of poverty; for no doubt the brother of your lady-mother would never abandon you."

"He died in Silesia."

"When?"

"Two years ago, I believe."

"You have been deceived, for I saw him at Stuttgart scarcely six months ago. He is the Baron de Treiden."

It did not cost me much to get wind of the adventurer, but I felt angry that he had had the impudence to try and dupe me. If it had not been for that I would willingly have given him six louis, for it would have been bad form on my part to declare war against adventurers, as I was one myself, and I ought to have pardoned his lies as nearly all adventurers are more or less impostors. I gave a glance at his diamond buckles, which were considered real at Grenoble, and I saw directly that they were counterfeits of a kind made in Venice, which imitate the facets of the diamonds in perfection, except to people who are experienced in diamonds.

"You have diamond buckles," said I. "Why don't you sell them?"

"It's the last piece of jewellery I possess out of all my mother gave me, and I promised her never to part with them."

"I would not shew those buckles if I were you; your pocket would be a better place for them. I may tell you frankly that I believe the stones to be counterfeit, and that your lie displeases me."

"Sir, I am not a liar."

"We shall see. Prove that the stones are genuine, and I will give you six louis. I shall be delighted if I am in the wrong. Farewell."

Seeing M. de Valerlglard coming up to my door, he begged me not to tell him of what had passed between us; and I promised that I would tell no one.

Valenglard came to wish me a prosperous journey; he himself was obliged to go with M. Monteinard. He begged me to correspond constantly with him, and I had been intending to prefer the same request, as I took too great an interest in the fair Mdlle. Roman not to wish to hear of her fate, and the correspondence the worthy officer desired was the best way possible for me to hear about her. As will be imagined, I promised what he asked without making any difficulty. He shed tears as he embraced me, and I promised to be his friend.

CHAPTER II

My Departure from Grenoble—Avignon—The Fountain of Vaucluse—The   False Astrodi and the Humpback—Gaetan Costa—I Arrive at Marseilles

While the three girls were helping Le Duc to pack my mails my landlord entered, gave me his bill, and finding everything correct I paid him, much to his satisfaction. I owed him a compliment, too, at which he seemed extremely gratified.

"Sir," said I, "I do not wish to leave your house without having the pleasure of dining with your charming girls, to shew them how I appreciate the care they have taken of me. Let me have, then, a delicate repast for four, and also order post horses, that I may start in the evening."

"Sir," broke in Le Duc, "I entreat you to order a saddle-horse besides; I was not made for a seat behind a chaise."

The cousin laughed openly at his vain boasting, and to avenge himself the rascal told her that he was better than she.

"Nevertheless, M. le Duc, you will have to wait on her at table."

"Yes, as she waits on you in bed."

I ran for my stick, but the rogue, knowing what was going to happen, opened the window and jumped into the courtyard. The girls gave a shriek of terror, but when we looked out we saw him jumping about and performing a thousand apish tricks.

Very glad to find that he had not broken a limb, I called out, "Come back, I forgive you." The girls, and the man himself who escaped so readily, were as delighted as I. Le Duc came in in high spirits, observing that he did not know he was such a good jumper.

"Very good, but don't be so impudent another time. Here, take this watch."

So saying, I gave him a valuable gold watch, which he received, saying,—

"I would jump again for another watch like this."

Such was my Spaniard, whom I had to dismiss two years afterwards. I have often missed him.

The hours went by with such speed when I was seated at table with the three girls, whom I vainly endeavoured to intoxicate, that I decided that I would not leave till the next day. I was tired of making mysteries and wanted to enjoy them all together, and resolved that the orgy should take place that night. I told them that if they would pass the night in my room I would not go till the next day. This proposition was received with a storm of exclamations and with laughter, as at an impossibility, while I endeavoured to excite them to grant my request. In the midst of this the door-keeper came in, advising me not to travel by night, but to go to Avignon by a boat in which I could ship my carriage.

"You will save time and money," said he.

"I will do so," I answered, "if these girls of yours will keep me company all night, as I am determined I will not go to bed."

"O Lord!" said he with a laugh, "that's their business."

This decided them and they gave in. The door-keeper sent to order the boat, and promised to let me have a dainty supper by midnight.

The hours passed by in jests and merriment, and when we sat down to supper I made the champagne corks fly to such an extent that the girls began to get rather gay. I myself felt a little heated, and as I held each one's secret I had the hardihood to tell them that their scruples were ridiculous, as each of them had shewn no reserve to me in private.

At this they gazed at one another in a kind of blank surprise, as if indignant at what I had said. Foreseeing that feminine pride might prompt them to treat my accusation as an idle calumny, I resolved not to give them time, and drawing Manon on to my knee I embraced her with such ardour that she gave in and abandoned herself to my passion. Her example overcame the others, and for five hours we indulged in every kind of voluptuous enjoyment. At the end of that time we were all in need of rest, but I had to go. I wanted to give them some jewels, but they said they would rather I ordered gloves to the amount of thirty louis, the money to be paid in advance, and the gloves not to be called for.

I went to sleep on board the boat, and did not awake till we got to Avignon. I was conducted to the inn of "St. Omen" and supped in my room in spite of the marvellous tales which Le Duc told me of a young beauty at the public table.

Next morning my Spaniard told me that the beauty and her husband slept in a room next to mine. At the same time he brought me a bill of the play, and I saw Company from Paris, with Mdlle. Astrodi, who was to sing and dance. I gave a cry of wonder, and exclaimed,—

"The famous Astrodi at Avignon—how she will be astonished to see me!"

Not wanting to live in hermit fashion, I went downstairs to dine at the public table, and I found a score of people sitting down to such a choice repast that I could not conceive how it could be done for forty sous a head. The fair stranger drew all eyes, and especially mine, towards her. She was a young and perfect beauty, silent, her eyes fixed on a napkin, replying in monosyllables to those who addressed her, and glancing at the speaker with large blue eyes, the beauty of which it would be difficult to describe. Her husband was seated at the other end of the table—a man of a kind that inspires contempt at the first glance. He was young, marked with the small-pox, a greedy eater, a loud talker, laughing and speaking at random, and altogether I took him for a servant in disguise. Feeling sure that such a fellow did not know how to refuse, I sent him a glass of champagne, which he drank off to my health forthwith. "May I have the pleasure of sending a glass to your wife?" He replied, with a roar of laughter, to ask her myself; and with a slight bow she told me that she never took anything to drink. When the dessert came in she rose, and her husband followed her to their room.

A stranger who like myself had never seen her before, asked me who she was. I said I was a newcomer and did not know, and somebody else said that her husband called himself the Chevalier Stuard, that he came from Lyons, and was going to Marseilles; he came, it appeared, to Avignon a week ago, without servants, and in a very poor carriage.

I intended staying at Avignon only as long as might be necessary to see the Fountain or Fall of Vaucluse, and so I had not got any letters of introduction, and had not the pretext of acquaintance that I might stay and enjoy her fine eyes. But an Italian who had read and enjoyed the divine Petrarch would naturally wish to see the place made divine by the poet's love for Laura. I went to the theatre, where I saw the vice-legate Salviati, women of fashion, neither fair nor foul, and a wretched comic opera; but I neither saw Astrodi nor any other actor from the Comedie Italienne at Paris.

"Where is the famous Astrodi?" said I, to a young man sitting by me, "I have not seen her yet."

"Excuse me, she has danced and sang before your eyes."

"By Jove, it's impossible! I know her perfectly, and if she has so changed as not to be recognized she is no longer herself."

I turned to go, and two minutes after the young man I had addressed came up and begged me to come back, and he would take me to Astradi's dressing-room, as she had recognized me. I followed him without saying a word, and saw a plain-looking girl, who threw her arms round my neck and addressed me by my name, though I could have sworn I had never seen her before, but she did not leave me time to speak. Close by I saw a man who gave himself out as the father of the famous Astrodi, who was known to all Paris, who had caused the death of the Comte d'Egmont, one of the most amiable noblemen of the Court of Louis XV. I thought this ugly female might be her sister, so I sat down and complimented her on her talents. She asked if I would mind her changing her dress; and in a moment she was running here and there, laughing and shewing a liberality which possibly might have been absent if what she had to display had been worth seeing.

I laughed internally at her wiles, for after my experiences at Grenoble she would have found it a hard task to arouse my desires if she had been as pretty as she was ugly. Her thinness and her tawny skin could not divert my attention from other still less pleasing features about her. I admired her confidence in spite of her disadvantages. She must have credited me with a diabolic appetite, but these women often contrive to extract charms out of their depravity which their delicacy would be impotent to furnish. She begged me to sup with her, and as she persisted I was obliged to refuse her in a way I should not have allowed myself to use with any other woman. She then begged me to take four tickets for the play the next day, which was to be for her benefit. I saw it was only a matter of twelve francs, and delighted to be quit of her so cheaply I told her to give me sixteen. I thought she would have gone mad with joy when I gave her a double louis. She was not the real Astrodi. I went back to my inn and had a delicious supper in my own room.

While Le Duc was doing my hair before I went to bed, he told me that the landlord had paid a visit to the fair stranger and her husband before supper, and had said in clear terms that he must be paid next morning; and if he were not, no place would be laid for them at table, and their linen would be detained.

"Who told you that?"

"I heard it from here; their room is only separated from this by a wooden partition. If they were in it now, I am sure they could hear all we are saying."

"Where are they, then?"

"At table, where they are eating for to-morrow, but the lady is crying.
There's a fine chance for you, sir."

"Be quiet; I shan't have anything to do with it. It's a trap, for a woman of any worth would die rather than weep at a public table."

"Ah, if you saw how pretty she looks in tears! I am only a poor devil, but I would willingly give her two louis if she would earn them."

"Go and offer her the money."

A moment after the gentleman and his wife came back to their room, and I heard the loud voice of the one and the sobs of the other, but as he was speaking Walloon I did not understand what he said.

"Go to bed," said I to Le Duc, "and next morning tell the landlord to get me another room, for a wooden partition is too thin a barrier to keep off people whom despair drive to extremities."

I went to bed myself, and the sobs and muttering did not die away till midnight.

I was shaving next morning, when Le Duc announced the Chevalier Stuard.

"Say I don't know anybody of that name."

He executed my orders, and returned saying that the chevalier on hearing my refusal to see him had stamped with rage, gone into his chamber, and come out again with his sword beside him.

"I am going to see," added Le Duc, "that your pistols are well primed for the future."

I felt inclined to laugh, but none the less I admired the foresight of my
Spaniard, for a man in despair is capable of anything.

"Go," said I, "and ask the landlord to give me another room."

In due course the landlord came himself and told me that he could not oblige me until the next day.

"If you don't get me another room I shall leave your house on the spot, because I don't like hearing sobs and reproaches all night."

"Can you hear them, sir?"

"You can hear them yourself now. What do you think of it? The woman will kill herself, and you will be the cause of her death."

"I, sir? I have only asked them to pay me my just debts."

"Hush! there goes the husband. I am sure he is telling his wife in his language that you are an unfeeling monster."

"He may tell her what he likes so long as he pays me."

"You have condemned them to die of hunger. How much do they owe you?"

"Fifty francs."

"Aren't you ashamed of making such a row for a wretched sum like that?"

"Sir, I am only ashamed of an ill deed, and I do not commit such a deed in asking for my own."

"There's your money. Go and tell them that you have been paid, and that they may eat again; but don't say who gave you the money."

"That's what I call a good action," said the fellow; and he went and told them that they did not owe him anything, but that they would never know who paid the money.

"You may dine and sup," he added, "at the public table, but you must pay me day by day."

After he had delivered this speech in a high voice, so that I could hear as well as if I had been in the room, he came back to me.

"You stupid fool!" said I, pushing him away, "they will know everything."
So saying I shut my door.

Le Duc stood in front of me, staring stupidly before him.

"What's the matter with you, idiot?" said I.

"That's fine. I see. I am going on the stage. You would do well to become an actor."

"You are a fool."

"Not so big a fool as you think."

"I am going for a walk; mind you don't leave my room for a moment."

I had scarcely shut the door when the chevalier accosted me and overwhelmed me with thanks.

"Sir, I don't know to what you are referring."

He thanked me again and left me, and walking by the banks of the Rhone, which geographers say is the most rapid river in Europe, I amused myself by looking at the ancient bridge. At dinner-time I went back to the inn, and as the landlord knew that I paid six francs a meal he treated me to an exquisite repast. Here, I remember, I had some exceedingly choice Hermitage. It was so delicious that I drank nothing else. I wished to make a pilgrimage to Vaucluse and begged the landlord to procure me a good guide, and after I had dressed I went to the theatre.

I found the Astrodi at the door, and giving her my sixteen tickets, I sat down near the box of the vice-legate Salviati, who came in a little later, surrounded by a numerous train of ladies and gentlemen bedizened with orders and gold lace.

The so-called father of the false Astrodi came and whispered that his daughter begged me to say that she was the celebrated Astrodi I had known at Paris. I replied, also in a whisper, that I would not run the risk of being posted as a liar by bolstering up an imposture. The ease with which a rogue invites a gentleman to share in a knavery is astonishing; he must think his confidence confers an honour.

At the end of the first act a score of lackeys in the prince's livery took round ices to the front boxes. I thought it my duty to refuse. A young gentleman, as fair as love, came up to me, and with easy politeness asked me why I had refused an ice.

"Not having the honour to know anyone here, I did not care that anyone should be able to say that he had regaled one who was unknown to him."

"But you, sir, are a man who needs no introduction."

"You do me too much honour."

"You are staying at the 'St. Omer'!"

"Yes; I am only stopping here to see Vaucluse, where I think of going to-morrow if I can get a good guide."

"If you would do me the honour of accepting me, I should be delighted. My name is Dolci, I am son of the captain of the vice-legate's guard."

"I feel the honour you do me, and I accept your obliging offer. I will put off my start till your arrival."

"I will be with you at seven."

I was astonished at the easy grace of this young Adonis, who might have been a pretty girl if the tone of his voice had not announced his manhood. I laughed at the false Astrodi, whose acting was as poor as her face, and who kept staring at me all the time. While she sang she regarded me with a smile and gave me signs of an understanding, which must have made the audience notice me, and doubtless pity my bad taste. The voice and eyes of one actress pleased me; she was young and tall, but hunchbacked to an extraordinary degree. She was tall in spite of her enormous humps, and if it had not been for this malformation she would have been six feet high. Besides her pleasing eyes and very tolerable voice I fancied that, like all hunchbacks, she was intelligent. I found her at the door with the ugly Astrodi when I was leaving the theatre. The latter was waiting to thank me, and the other was selling tickets for her benefit.

After the Astrodi had thanked me, the hunchbacked girl turned towards me, and with a smile that stretched from ear to ear and displayed at least twenty-four exquisite teeth, she said that she hoped I would honour her by being present at her benefit.

"If I don't leave before it comes off, I will," I replied.

At this the impudent Astrodi laughed, and in the hearing of several ladies waiting for their carriages told me that her friend might be sure of my presence, as she would not let me go before the benefit night. "Give him sixteen tickets," she added. I was ashamed to refuse, and gave her two louis. Then in a lower voice the Astrodi said, "After the show we will come and sup with you, but on the condition that you ask nobody else, as we want to be alone."

In spite of a feeling of anger, I thought that such a supper-party would be amusing, and as no one in the town knew me I resolved to stay in the hope of enjoying a hearty laugh.

I was having my supper when Stuard and his wife went to their room. This night I heard no sobs nor reproaches, but early next morning I was surprised to see the chevalier who said, as if we had been old friends, that he had heard that I was going to Vaucluse, and that as I had taken a carriage with four places he would be much obliged if I would allow him and his wife, who wanted to see the fountain, to go with me. I consented.

Le Duc begged to be allowed to accompany me on horseback, saying that he had been a true prophet. In fact it seemed as if the couple had agreed to repay me for my expenditure by giving me new hopes. I was not displeased with the expedition, and it was all to my advantage, as I had had recourse to no stratagems to obtain it.

Dolci came, looking as handsome as an angel; my neighbours were ready, and the carriage loaded with the best provisions in food and drink that were obtainable; and we set off, Dolci seated beside the lady and I beside the chevalier.

I had thought that the lady's sadness would give place, if not to gaiety, at least to a quiet cheerfulness, but I was mistaken; for, to all my remarks, grave or gay, she replied, either in monosyllables or in a severely laconic style. Poor Dolci, who was full of wit, was stupefied. He thought himself the cause of her melancholy, and was angry with himself for having innocently cast a shadow on the party of pleasure. I relieved him of his fears by telling him that when he offered me his pleasant society I was not aware that I was to be of service to the fair lady. I added that when at day-break I received this information, I was pleased that he would have such good company. The lady did not say a word. She kept silent and gloomy all the time, and gazed to right and left like one who does not see what is before his [her] eyes.

Dolci felt at ease after my explanation, and did his best to arouse the lady, but without success. He talked on a variety of topics to the husband, always giving her an opportunity of joining in, but her lips remained motionless. She looked like the statue of Pandora before it had been quickened by the divine flame.

The beauty of her face was perfect; her eyes were of a brilliant blue, her complexion a delicate mixture of white and red, her arms were as rounded as a Grace's, her hands plump and well shaped, her figure was that of a nymph's, giving delightful hints of a magnificent breast; her hair was a chestnut brown, her foot small:

she had all that constitutes a beautiful woman save that gift of intellect, which makes beauty more beautiful, and gives a charm to ugliness itself. My vagrant fancy shewed me her naked form, all seemed ravishing, and yet I thought that though she might inspire a passing fancy she could not arouse a durable affection. She might minister to a man's pleasures, she could not make him happy. I arrived at the isle resolved to trouble myself about her no more; she might, I thought, be mad, or in despair at finding herself in the power of a man whom she could not possibly love. I could not help pitying her, and yet I could not forgive her for consenting to be of a party which she knew she must spoil by her morose behaviour.

As for the self-styled Chevalier Stuard, I did not trouble my head whether he were her husband or her lover. He was young, commonplace-looking, he spoke affectedly; his manners were not good, and his conversation betrayed both ignorance and stupidity. He was a beggar, devoid of money and wits, and I could not make out why he took with him a beauty who, unless she were over-kind, could add nothing to his means of living. Perhaps he expected to live at the expense of simpletons, and had come to the conclusion, in spite of his ignorance, that the world is full of such; however, experience must have taught him that this plan cannot be relied on.

When we got to Vaucluse I let Dolci lead; he had been there a hundred times, and his merit was enhanced in my eyes by the fact that he was a lover of the lover of Laura. We left the carriage at Apt, and wended our way to the fountain which was honoured that day with a numerous throng of pilgrims. The stream pours forth from a vast cavern, the handiwork of nature, inimitable by man. It is situated at the foot of a rock with a sheer descent of more than a hundred feet. The cavern is hardly half as high, and the water pours forth from it in such abundance that it deserves the name of river at its source. It is the Sorgue which falls into the Rhone near Avignon. There is no other stream as pure and clear, for the rocks over which it flows harbour no deposits of any kind. Those who dislike it on account of its apparent blackness should remember that the extreme darkness of the cavern gives it that gloomy tinge.

> Chiare fresche a dolce aque
> Ove le belle membra
> Pose colei the sola a me pay donna.

I wished to ascend to that part of the rock where Petrarch's house stood. I gazed on the remains with tears in my eyes, like Leo Allatius at Homer's grave. Sixteen years later I slept at Arqua, where Petrarch died, and his house still remains. The likeness between the two situations was astonishing, for from Petrarch's study at Arqua a rock can be seen similar to that which may be viewed at Vaucluse; this was the residence of Madonna Laura.

"Let us go there," said I, "it is not far off."

I will not endeavour to delineate my feelings as I contemplated the ruins of the house where dwelt the lady whom the amorous Petrarch immortalised in his verse—verse made to move a heart of stone:

"Morte bella parea nel suo bel viso"

I threw myself with arms outstretched upon the ground as if I would embrace the very stones. I kissed them, I watered them with my tears, I strove to breathe the holy breath they once contained. I begged Madame Stuard's pardon for having left her arm to do homage to the spirit of a woman who had quickened the profoundest soul that ever lived.

I say soul advisedly, for after all the body and the senses had nothing to do with the connection.

"Four hundred years have past and gone," said I to the statue of a woman who gazed at me in astonishment, "since Laura de Sade walked here; perhaps she was not as handsome as you, but she was lively, kindly, polite, and good of heart. May this air which she breathed and which you breathe now kindle in you the spark of fire divine; that fire that coursed through her veins, and made her heart beat and her bosom swell. Then you would win the worship of all worthy men, and from none would you receive the least offence. Gladness, madam, is the lot of the happy, and sadness the portion of souls condemned to everlasting pains. Be cheerful, then, and you will do something to deserve your beauty."

The worthy Dolci was kindled by my enthusiasm. He threw himself upon me, and kissed me again and again; the fool Stuard laughed; and his wife, who possibly thought me mad, did not evince the slightest emotion. She took my arm, and we walked slowly towards the house of Messer Francesco d'Arezzo, where I spent a quarter of an hour in cutting my name. After that we had our dinner.

Dolci lavished more attention on the extraordinary woman than I did. Stuard did nothing but eat and drink, and despised the Sorgue water, which, said he, would spoil the Hermitage; possibly Petrarch may have been of the same opinion. We drank deeply without impairing our reason, but the lady was very temperate. When we reached Avignon we bade her farewell, declining the invitation of her foolish husband to come and rest in his rooms.

I took Dolci's arm and we walked beside the Rhone as the sun went down.

Among other keen and witty observations the young man said,—

"That woman is an old hand, infatuated with a sense of her own merit. I would bet that she has only left her own country because her charms, from being too freely displayed, have ceased to please there. She must be sure of making her fortune out of anybody she comes across. I suspect that the fellow who passes for her husband is a rascal, and that her pretended melancholy is put on to drive a persistent lover to distraction. She has not yet succeeded in finding a dupe, but as she will no doubt try to catch a rich man, it is not improbable that she is hovering over you.".

When a young man of Dolci's age reasons like that, he is bound to become a great master. I kissed him as I bade him good-night, thanked him for his kindness, and we agreed that we would see more of one another.

As I came back to my inn I was accosted by a fine-looking man of middle age, who greeted me by name and asked with great politeness if I had found Vaucluse as fine as I had expected. I was delighted to recognize the Marquis of Grimaldi, a Genoese, a clever and good-natured man, with plenty of money, who always lived at Venice because he was more at liberty to enjoy himself there than in his native country; which shews that there is no lack of freedom at Venice.

After I had answered his question I followed him into his room, where having exhausted the subject of the fountain he asked me what I thought of my fair companion.

"I did not find her satisfactory in all respects," I answered; and noticing the reserve with which I spoke, he tried to remove it by the following confession:

"There are some very pretty women in Genoa, but not one to compare with her whom you took to Vaucluse to-day. I sat opposite to her at table yesterday evening, and I was struck with her perfect beauty. I offered her my arm up the stair; I told her that I was sorry to see her so sad, and if I could do anything for her she had only to speak. You know I was aware she had no money. Her husband, real or pretended, thanked me for my offer, and after I had wished them a good night I left them.

"An hour ago you left her and her husband at the door of their apartment, and soon afterwards I took the liberty of calling. She welcomed me with a pretty bow, and her husband went out directly, begging me to keep her company till his return. The fair one made no difficulty in sitting next to me on a couch, and this struck me as a good omen, but when I took her hand she gently drew it away. I then told, her, in as few words as I could, that her beauty had made me in love with her, and that if she wanted a hundred louis they were at her service, if she would drop her melancholy, and behave in a manner suitable to the feelings with which she had inspired me. She only replied by a motion of the head, which shewed gratitude, but also an absolute refusal of my offer. 'I am going to-morrow,' said I. No answer. I took her hand again, and she drew it back with an air of disdain which wounded me. I begged her to excuse me, and I left the room without more ado.

"That's an account of what happened an hour ago. I am not amorous of her, it was only a whim; but knowing, as I do, that she has no money, her manner astonished me. I fancied that you might have placed her in a position to despise my offer, and this would explain her conduct, in a measure; otherwise I can't understand it at all. May I ask you to tell me whether you are more fortunate than I?"

I was enchanted with the frankness of this noble gentleman, and did not hesitate to tell him all, and we laughed together at our bad fortune: I had to promise to call on him at Genoa, and tell him whatever happened between us during the two days I purposed to remain at Avignon. He asked me to sup with him and admire the fair recalcitrant.

"She has had an excellent dinner," said I, "and in all probability she will not have any supper."

"I bet she will," said the marquis; and he was right, which made me see clearly that the woman was playing a part. A certain Comte de Bussi, who had just come, was placed next to her at table. He was a good-looking young man with a fatuous sense of his own superiority, and he afforded us an amusing scene.

He was good-natured, a wit, and inclined to broad jokes, and his manner towards women bordered on the impudent. He had to leave at midnight and began to make love to his fair neighbour forthwith, and teased her in a thousand ways; but she remained as dumb as a statue, while he did all the talking and laughing, not regarding it within the bounds of possibility that she might be laughing at him.

I looked at M. Grimaldi, who found it as difficult to keep his countenance as I did. The young roue was hurt at her silence, and continued pestering her, giving her all the best pieces on his plate after tasting them first. The lady refused to take them, and he tried to put them into her mouth, while she repulsed him in a rage. He saw that no one seemed inclined to take her part, and determined to continue the assault, and taking her hand he kissed it again and again. She tried to draw it away, and as she rose he put his arm round her waist and made her sit down on his knee; but at this point the husband took her arm and led her out of the room. The attacking party looked rather taken aback for a moment as he followed her with his eyes, but sat down again and began to eat and laugh afresh, while everybody else kept a profound silence. He then turned to the footman behind his chair and asked him if his sword was upstairs. The footman said no, and then the fatuous young man turned to an abbe who sat near me, and enquired who had taken away his mistress:

"It was her husband," said the abbe.

"Her husband! Oh, that's another thing; husbands don't fight—a man of honour always apologises to them."

With that he got up, went upstairs, and came down again directly, saying,—

"The husband's a fool. He shut the door in my face, and told me to satisfy my desires somewhere else. It isn't worth the trouble of stopping, but I wish I had made an end of it."

He then called for champagne, offered it vainly to everybody, bade the company a polite farewell and went upon his way.

As M. Grimaldi escorted me to my room he asked me what I had thought of the scene we had just witnessed. I told him I would not have stirred a finger, even if he had turned up her clothes.

"No more would I," said he, "but if she had accepted my hundred louis it would have been different. I am curious to know the further history of this siren, and I rely upon you to tell me all about it as you go through Genoa."

He went away at day-break next morning.

When I got up I received a note from the false Astrodi, asking me if I expected her and her great chum to supper. I had scarcely replied in the affirmative, when the sham Duke of Courland I had left at Grenoble appeared on the scene. He confessed in a humble voice that he was the son of clock-maker at Narva, that his buckles were valueless, and that he had come to beg an alms of me. I gave him four louis, and he asked me to keep his secret. I replied that if anyone asked me about him that I should say what was absolutely true, that I knew him nothing about him. "Thank you; I am now going to Marseilles." "I hope you will have a prosperous journey." Later on my readers will hear how I found him at Genoa. It is a good thing to know something about people of his kind, of whom there are far too many in the world.

I called up the landlord and told him I wanted a delicate supper for three in my own room.

He told me that I should have it, and then said, "I have just had a row with the Chevalier Stuard."

"What about?"

"Because he has nothing to pay me with, and I am going to turn them out immediately, although the lady is in bed in convulsions which are suffocating her."

"Take out your bill in her charms."

"Ah, I don't care for that sort of thing! I am getting on in life, and I don't want any more scenes to bring discredit on my house."

"Go and tell her that from henceforth she and her husband will dine and sup in their own room and that I will pay for them as long as I remain here."

"You are very generous, sir, but you know that meals in a private room are charged double."

"I know they are."

"Very good."

I shuddered at the idea of the woman being turned out of doors without any resources but her body, by which she refused to profit. On the other hand I could not condemn the inn-keeper who, like his fellows, was not troubled with much gallantry. I had yielded to an impulse of pity without any hopes of advantage for myself. Such were my thoughts when Stuard came to thank me, begging me to come and see his wife and try and persuade her to behave in a different manner.

"She will give me no answers, and you know that that sort of thing is rather tedious."

"Come, she knows what you have done for her; she will talk to you, for her feelings . . . ."

"What business have you to talk about feelings after what happened yesterday evening?"

"It was well for that gentleman that he went away at midnight, otherwise
I should have killed him this morning."

"My dear sir, allow me to tell you that all that is pure braggadocio. Yesterday, not to-day, was the time to kill him, or to throw your plate at his head, at all events. We will now go and see your wife."

I found her in bed, her face to the wall, the coverlet right up to her chin, and her body convulsed with sobs. I tried to bring her to reason, but as usual got no reply. Stuard wanted to leave me, but I told him that if he went out I would go too, as I could do nothing to console her, as he might know after her refusing the Marquis of Grimaldi's hundred louis for a smile and her hand to kiss.

"A hundred Louis!" cried the fellow with a sturdy oath; "what folly! We might have been at home at Liege by now. A princess allows one to kiss her hand for nothing, and she.... A hundred Louis! Oh, damnable!"

His exclamations, very natural under the circumstances, made me feel inclined to laugh. The poor devil swore by all his gods, and I was about to leave the room, when all at once the wretched woman was seized with true or false convulsions. With one hand she seized a water-bottle and sent it flying into the middle of the room, and with the other she tore the clothes away from her breast. Stuard tried to hold her, but her disorder increased in violence, and the coverlet was disarranged to such a degree that I could see the most exquisite naked charms imaginable. At last she grew calm, and her eyes closed as if exhausted; she remained in the most voluptuous position that desire itself could have invented. I began to get very excited. How was I to look on such beauties without desiring to possess them? At this point her wretched husband left the room, saying he was gone to fetch some water. I saw the snare, and my self-respect prevented my being caught in it. I had an idea that the whole scene had been arranged with the intent that I should deliver myself up to brutal pleasure, while the proud and foolish woman would be free to disavow all participation in the fact. I constrained myself, and gently veiled what I would fain have revealed in all its naked beauty. I condemned to darkness these charms which this monster of a woman only wished me to enjoy that I might be debased.

Stuard was long enough gone. When he came back with the water-bottle full, he was no doubt surprised to find me perfectly calm, and in no disorder of any kind, and a few minutes afterwards I went out to cool myself by the banks of the Rhone.

I walked along rapidly, feeling enraged with myself, for I felt that the woman had bewitched me. In vain I tried to bring myself to reason; the more I walked the more excited I became, and I determined that after what I had seen the only cure for my disordered fancy was enjoyment, brutal or not. I saw that I should have to win her, not by an appeal to sentiment but by hard cash, without caring what sacrifices I made. I regretted my conduct, which then struck me in the light of false delicacy, for if I had satisfied my desires and she chose to turn prude, I might have laughed her to scorn, and my position would have been unassailable. At last I determined on telling the husband that I would give him twenty-five louis if he could obtain me an interview in which I could satisfy my desires.

Full of this idea I went back to the inn, and had my dinner in my own room without troubling to enquire after her. Le Duc told me that she was dining in her room too, and that the landlord had told the company that she would not take her meals in public any more. This was information I possessed already.

After dinner I called on the good-natured Dolci, who introduced me to his father, an excellent man, but not rich enough to satisfy his son's desire of travelling. The young man was possessed of considerable dexterity, and performed a number of very clever conjuring tricks. He had an amiable nature, and seeing that I was curious to know about his love affairs he told me numerous little stories which shewed me that he was at that happy age when one's inexperience is one's sole misfortune.

There was a rich lady for whom he did not care, as she wanted him to give her that which he would be ashamed to give save for love, and there was a girl who required him to treat her with respect. I thought I could give him a piece of good advice, so I told him to grant his favours to the rich woman, and to fail in respect now and again to the girl, who would be sure to scold and then forgive. He was no profligate, and seemed rather inclined to become a Protestant. He amused himself innocently with his friends of his own age, in a garden near Avignon, and a sister of the gardener's wife was kind to him when they were alone.

In the evening I went back to the inn, and I had not long to wait for the Astrodi and the Lepi (so the hunchbacked girl was named); but when I saw these two caricatures of women I felt stupefied. I had expected them, of course, but the reality confounded me. The Astrodi tried to counterbalance her ugliness by an outrageous freedom of manners; while the Lepi, who though a hunchback was very talented and an excellent actress, was sure of exciting desire by the rare beauty of her eyes and teeth, which latter challenged admiration from her enormous mouth by their regularity and whiteness. The Astrodi rushed up to me and gave me an Italian embrace, to which, willy nilly, I was obliged to submit. The quieter Lepi offered me her cheek, which I pretended to kiss. I saw that the Astrodi was in a fair way to become intolerable, so I begged her to moderate her transports, because as a novice at these parties I wanted to get accustomed to them by degrees. She promised that she would be very good.

While we were waiting for supper I asked her, for the sake of something to say, whether she had found a lover at Avignon.

"Only the vice-legate's auditor," she replied; "and though he makes me his pathic he is good-natured and generous. I have accustomed myself to his taste easily enough, though I should have thought such a thing impossible a year ago, as I fancied the exercise a harmful one, but I was wrong."

"So the auditor makes a boy of you?"

"Yes. My sister would have adored him, as that sort of love is her passion."

"But your sister has such fine haunches."

"So have I! Look here, feel me."

"You are right; but wait a bit, it is too soon for that kind of thing yet."

"We will be wanton after supper."

"I think you are wanton now," said the Lepi.

"Why?"

"Why? Ought you to shew your person like that?"

"My dear girl, you will be shewing yourself soon. When one is in good company, one is in the golden age."

"I wonder at your telling everyone what sort of a connection you have with the auditor," said I.

"Nonsense! I don't tell everyone, but everyone tells me and congratulates me too. They know the worthy man never cared for women, and it would be absurd to deny what everybody guesses. I used to be astonished at my sister, but the best plan in this world is to be astonished at nothing. But don't you like that?"

"No, I only like this."

As I spoke I laid hands on the Lepi, on the spot where one usually finds what I called "this;" but the Astrodi, seeing that I found nothing, burst into a roar of laughter, and taking my hand put it just under her front hump, where at last I found what I wanted. The reader will guess my surprise. The poor creature, too ashamed to be prudish, laughed too. My spirits also begin to rise, as I thought of the pleasure I should get out of this new discovery after supper.

"Have you never had a lover?" said I to the Lepi.

"No," said the Astrodi, "she is still a maid."

"No, I am not," replied the Lepi, in some confusion, "I had a lover at Bordeaux, and another at Montpellier."

"Yes, I know, but you are still as you were born."

"I can't deny it."

"What's that? Two lovers and still a maid! I don't understand; please tell me about it, for I have never heard of such a thing."

"Before I satisfied my first lover which happened when I was only twelve,
I was just the same as I am now."

"It's wonderful. And what did he say when he saw it?"

"I swore that he was my first, and he believed me, putting it down to the peculiar shape of my body."

"He was a man of spirit; but didn't he hurt you?"

"Not a bit; but then he was very gentle."

"You must have a try after supper," said the Astrodi to me, "that would be fine fun."

"No, no," said the Lepi, "the gentleman would be too big for me."

"Nonsense! You don't want to take in all of him. I will show you how it is."

With these words the impudent hussy proceeded to exhibit me, and I let her do what she liked.

"That's just what I should have thought," cried the Lepi; "it could never be done."

"Well, he is rather big," answered the Astrodi; "but there's a cure for everything, and he will be content with half-measures."

"It's not the length, my dear, but the thickness which frightens me; I am afraid the door is too narrow."

"All the better for you, for you can sell your maidenhead after having had two lovers."

This conversation, not devoid of wit, and still more the simplicity of the hunchback, had made me resolve to verify things for myself.

Supper came up, and I had the pleasure of seeing the two nymphs eat like starving savages, and drink still better. When the Hermitage had done its work the Astrodi proposed that we should cast off the clothes which disfigure nature.

"Certainly," said I; "and I will turn away while you are getting ready."

I went behind the curtains, took off my clothes, and went to bed with my back to them. At last the Astrodi told me that they were ready, and when I looked the Lepi took up all my attention. In spite of her double deformity she was a handsome woman. My glances frightened her, for she was doubtless taking part in an orgy for the first time. I gave her courage, however, by dint of praising those charms which the white and beautiful hands could not hide, and at last I persuaded her to come and lie beside me. Her hump prevented her lying on her back, but the ingenious Astrodi doubled up the pillows and succeeded in placing her in a position similar to that of a ship about to be launched. It was also by the tender care of the Astrodi that the introduction of the knife was managed, to the great delight of priest and victim. After the operation was over she got up and kissed me, which she could not do before, for her mouth reached to the middle of my chest, while my feet were scarcely down to her knees. I would have given ten louis to have been able to see the curious sight we must have presented at work.

"Now comes my turn," said the Astrodi; "but I don't want you to infringe on the rights of my auditor, so come and look round and see where the path lies. Take that."

"What am I to do with this slice of lemon?"

"I want you to try whether the place is free from infection, or whether it would be dangerous for you to pay it a visit."

"Is that a sure method?"

"Infallible; if everything were not right I could not bear the smart."

"There you are. How's that?"

"All right; but don't deceive me, I want no half measures. My reputation would be made if I became with child."

I ask my reader's leave to draw a veil over some incidents of this truly scandalous orgy, in which the ugly woman taught me some things I did not know before. At last, more tired than exhausted, I told them to begone, but the Astrodi insisted on finishing up with a bowl of punch. I agreed, but not wishing to have anything more to do with either of them I dressed myself again. However, the champagne punch excited them to such an extent that at last they made me share their transports. The Astrodi placed her friend in such a singular position that the humps were no longer visible, and imagining that I had before me the high priestess of Jove, I paid her a long sacrifice, in which death and resurrection followed one another in succession. But I felt disgusted with myself, and drew away from their lascivious frenzies, and gave them ten Louis to get rid of them. The Astrodi fell on her knees, blessed me, thanked me, called me her god; and the Lepi wept and laughed for joy at the same time; and thus for a quarter of an hour I was treated to a scene of an extraordinary kind.

I had them taken home in my carriage, and slept till ten o'clock next morning. Just as I was going out for a walk Stuard came to my room and told me, with an air of despair, that if I did not give him the means of going away before I left he would throw himself in the Rhine.

"That's rather tragic," said I, "but I can find a cure. I will disburse twenty-five Louis, but it is your wife who must receive them; and the only condition is that she must receive me alone for an hour, and be entirely kind."

"Sir, we need just that sum; my wife is disposed to receive you; go and talk to her. I shall not be in till noon."

I put twenty-five Louis in a pretty little purse, and left my room thinking that the victory was won. I entered her room and approached her bed respectfully. When she heard me she sat up in bed without taking the trouble to cover her breast, and before I could wish her good-day she spoke to me as follows:

"I am ready, sir, to pay with my body for the wretched twenty-five Louis of which my husband is in need. You can do what you like with me; but remember that in taking advantage of my position to assuage your brutal lust you are the viler of the two, for I only sell myself so cheaply because necessity compels me to do so. Your baseness is more shameful than mine. Come on; here I am."

With this flattering address she threw off the coverlet with a vigorous gesture, and displayed all her beauties, which I might have gazed on with such different feelings from those which now filled my breast. For a moment I was silent with indignation. All my passion had evaporated; in those voluptuous rounded limbs I saw now only the covering of a wild beast's soul. I put back the coverlet with the greatest calmness, and addressed her in a tone of cold contempt:

"No, madam, I shall not leave this room degraded because you have told me so, but I shall leave it after imparting to you a few degrading truths, of which you cannot be ignorant if you are a woman of any decency whatever. Here are twenty-five louis, a wretched sum to give a virtuous woman in payment of her favours, but much more than you deserve. I am not brutal, and to convince you of the fact I am going to leave you in the undisturbed possession of your charms, which I despise as heartily as I should have admired them if your behaviour had been different. I only give you the money from a feeling of compassion which I cannot overcome, and which is the only feeling I now have for you. Nevertheless, let me tell you that whether a woman sells herself for twenty-five louis or twenty-five million louis she is as much a prostitute in the one case as in the other, if she does not give her love with herself, or at all events the semblance of love. Farewell."

I went back to my room, and in course of time Stuard came to thank me.

"Sir," said I, "let me alone; I wish to hear no more about your wife."

They went away the next day for Lyons, and my readers will hear of them again at Liege.

In the afternoon Dolci took me to his garden that I might see the gardener's sister. She was pretty, but not so pretty as he was. He soon got her into a good humour, and after some trifling objection she consented to be loved by him in my presence. I saw that this Adonis had been richly dowered by nature, and I told him that with such a physical conformation he had no need of emptying his father's purse to travel, and before long he took my advice. This fair Ganymede might easily have turned me into Jove, as he struggled amorously with the gardener's sister.

As I was going home I saw a young man coming out of a boat; he was from twenty to twenty-five years old, and looked very sad. Seeing me looking at him, he accosted me, and humbly asked for alms, shewing me a document authorizing him to beg, and a passport stating he had left Madrid six weeks before. He came from Parma, and was named Costa. When I saw Parma my national prejudice spoke in his favour, and I asked him what misfortune had reduced him to beggary.

"Only lack of money to return to my native country," said he.

"What were you doing at Madrid, and why did you leave?"

"I was there four years as valet to Dr. Pistoria, physician to the King of Spain, but on my health failing I left him. Here is a certificate which will shew you that I gave satisfaction."

"What can you do?"

"I write a good hand, I can assist a gentleman as his secretary, and I intend being a scribe when I get home. Here are some verses I copied yesterday."

"You write well; but can you write correctly without a book?"

"I can write from dictation in French, Latin, and Spanish."

"Correctly?"

"Yes, sir, if the dictation is done properly, for it is the business of the one who dictates to see that everything is correct."

I saw that Master Gaetan Costa was an ignoramus, but in spite of that I took him to my room and told Le Duc to address him in Spanish. He answered well enough, but on my dictating to him in Italian and French I found he had not the remotest ideas on orthography.

"But you can't write," said I to him. However, I saw he was mortified at this, and I consoled him by saying that I would take him to his own country at my expense. He kissed my hand, and assured me that I should find a faithful servant in him.

This young fellow took my fancy by his originality; he had probably assumed it to distinguish himself from the blockheads amongst whom he had hitherto lived, and now used it in perfect good faith with everybody. He thought that the art of a scribe solely consisted in possessing a good hand, and that the fairest writer would be the best scribe. He said as much while he was examining a paper I had written, and as my writing was not as legible as his he tacitly told me I was his inferior, and that I should therefore treat him with some degree of respect. I laughed at this fad, and, not thinking him incorrigible I took him into my service. If it had not been for that odd notion of his I should probably have merely given him a louis, and no more. He said that spelling was of no consequence, as those who knew how to spell could easily guess the words, while those who did not know were unable to pick out the mistakes. I laughed, but as I said nothing he thought the laugh signified approval. In the dictation I gave him the Council of Trent happened to occur. According to his system he wrote Trent by a three and a nought. I burst out laughing; but he was not in the least put out, only remarking that the pronunciation being the same it was of no consequence how the word was spelt. In point of fact this lad was a fool solely through his intelligence, matched with ignorance and unbounded self-confidence. I was pleased with his originality and kept him, and was thus the greater fool of the two, as the reader will see.

I left Avignon next day, and went straight to Marseilles, not troubling to stop at Aix. I halted at the "Treize Cantons," wishing to stay for a week at least in this ancient colony of the Phocaeans, and to do as I liked there. With this idea I took no letter of introduction; I had plenty of money, and needed nobody's help. I told my landlord to give me a choice fish dinner in my own room, as I was aware that the fish in those parts is better than anywhere else.

I went out the next morning with a guide, to take me back to the inn when I was tired of walking. Not heeding where I went, I reached a fine quay; I thought I was at Venice again, and I felt my bosom swell, so deeply is the love of fatherland graven on the heart of every good man. I saw a number of stalls where Spanish and Levantine wines were kept, and a number of people drinking in them. A crowd of business men went hither and thither, running up against each other, crossing each other's paths, each occupied with his own business, and not caring whose way he got into. Hucksters, well dressed and ill dressed, women, pretty and plain, women who stared boldly at everyone, modest maidens with downcast eyes, such was the picture I saw.

The mixture of nationalities, the grave Turk and the glittering Andalusian, the French dandy, the gross Negro, the crafty Greek, the dull Hollander; everything reminded me of Venice, and I enjoyed the scene.

I stopped a moment at a street corner to read a playbill, and then I went back to the inn and refreshed my weary body with a delicious dinner, washed down with choice Syracusan wine. After dinner I dressed and took a place in the amphitheatre of the theatre.

CHAPTER III

Rosalie—Toulon—Nice—I Arrive at Genoa—M. Grimaldi—Veronique and Her Sister

I noticed that the four principal boxes on both sides of the proscenium were adorned with pretty women, but not a single gentleman. In the interval between the first and second acts I saw gentlemen of all classes paying their devoirs to these ladies. Suddenly I heard a Knight of Malta say to a girl, who was the sole occupant of a box next to me,

"I will breakfast with you to-morrow."

This was enough for me. I looked at her more closely and finding her to be a dainty morsel I said, as soon as the knight had gone—

"Will you give me my supper?"

"With pleasure; but I have been taken in so often that I shan't expect you without an earnest."

"How can I give you an earnest? I don't understand."

"You must be a new-comer here."

"Just arrived."

She laughed, called the knight, and said,—

"Be pleased to explain to this gentleman, who has just asked me for supper, the meaning of the word 'earnest.'"

The good-natured knight explained, with a smile, that the lady, fearing lest my memory should prove defective, wanted me to pay for my supper in advance. I thanked him, and asked her if a louis would be enough; and on her replying in the affirmative, I gave her the Louis and asked for her address. The knight told me politely that he would take me there himself after the theatre, adding,—

"She's the wantonest wench in all Marseilles."

He then asked me if I knew the town, and when I told him that I had only come that day he said he was glad to be the first to make my acquaintance. We went to the middle of, the amphitheatre and he pointed out a score of girls to right and left, all of them ready to treat the first comer to supper. They are all on the free list, and the manager finds they serve his ends as respectable women will not sit in their boxes, and they draw people to the theatre. I noticed five or six of a better type than the one I had engaged, but I resolved to stick to her for the evening, and to make the acquaintance of the others another time.

"Is your favourite amongst them?" I said to the knight.

"No, I keep a ballet-girl, and I will introduce you to her, as I am glad to say that I am free from all jealousy."

When the play came to an end he took me to my nymph's lodging, and we parted with the understanding that we were to see more of one another.

I found the lady in undress—a circumstance which went against her, for what I saw did not please me. She gave me a capital supper, and enlivened me by some witty and wanton sallies which made me regard her in a more favourable light. When we had supper she got into bed, and asked me to follow her example; but I told her that I never slept out. She then offered me the English article which brings peace to the soul, but I did not accept the one she offered as I thought it looked of a common make.

"I have finer ones, but they are three francs each, and the maker only sells them by the dozen," she said. "I will take a dozen if they are really good," I replied.

She rang the bell, and a young, charming, and modest-looking girl came in. I was struck with her.

"You have got a nice maid," I remarked, when the girl had gone for the protective sheaths.

"She is only fifteen," she said, "and won't do anything, as she is new to it."

"Will you allow me to see for myself?"

"You may ask her if you like, but I don't think she will consent."

The girl came back with the packet, and putting myself in a proper position I told her to try one on. She proceeded to do so with a sulky air and with a kind of repugnance which made me feel interested in her. Number one would not go on, so she had to try on a second, and the result was that I besprinkled her plentifully. The mistress laughed, but she was indignant, threw the whole packet in my face, and ran away in a rage. I wanted nothing more after this, so I put the packet in my pocket, gave the woman two Louis, and left the room. The girl I had treated so cavalierly came to light me downstairs, and thinking I owed her an apology I gave her a Louis and begged her pardon. The poor girl was astonished, kissed my hand, and begged me to say nothing to her mistress.

"I will not, my dear, but tell me truly whether you are still a 'virgo intacta'."

"Certainly, sir!"

"Wonderful! but tell me why you wouldn't let me see for myself?"

"Because it revolted me."

"Nevertheless you will have to do so, for otherwise, in spite of your prettiness, people will not know what to make of you. Would you like to let me try?"

"Yes, but not in this horrible house."

"Where, then?"

"Go to my mother's to-morrow, I will be there. Your guide knows where she lives."

When I got outside, I asked the man if he knew her. He replied in the affirmative, and said he believed her to be an honest girl.

"You will take me to-morrow to see her mother," I said.

Next morning he took me to the end of the town, to a poor house, where I found a poor woman and poor children living on the ground floor, and eating hard black bread.

"What do you want?" said she.

"Is you daughter here?"

"No, and what if she were? I am not her bawd."

"No, of course not, my good woman."

Just then the girl came in, and the enraged mother flung an old pot which came handy, at her head. Luckily it missed, but she would not have escaped her mother's talons if I had not flung myself between them. However, the old woman set up a dismal shriek, the children imitated her, and the poor girl began to cry. This hubbub made my man come in.

"You hussy!" screamed the mother, "you are bringing disgrace on me; get out of my house. You are no longer my daughter!"

I was in a difficult position. The man begged her not to make such a noise, as it would draw all the neighbours about the house; but the enraged woman answered only by abuse. I drew six francs from my pocket and gave them to her, but she flung them in my face. At last I went out with the daughter, whose hair she attempted to pull out by the roots, which project was defeated by the aid of my man. As soon as we got outside, the mob which the uproar had attracted hooted me and followed me, and no doubt I should have been torn to pieces if I had not escaped into a church, which I left by another door a quarter of an hour later. My fright saved me, for I knew the ferocity of the Provencals, and I took care not to reply a word to the storm of abuse which poured on me. I believe that I was never in greater danger than on that day.

Before I got back to my inn I was rejoined by the servant and the girl.

"How could you lead me into such a dangerous position?" said I. "You must have known your mother was savage."

"I hoped she would behave respectfully to you."

"Be calm; don't weep any more. Tell me how I can serve you."

"Rather than return to that horrible house I was in yesterday I would throw myself into the sea."

"Do you know of any respectable house where I can keep her?" said I to the man.

He told me he did know a respectable individual who let furnished apartments.

"Take me to it, then."

The man was of an advanced age, and he had rooms to let on all the floors.

"I only want a little nook," said the girl; and the old man took us to the highest story, and opened the door of a garret, saying—

"This closet is six francs a month, a month's rent to be paid in advance, and I may tell you that my door is always shut at ten o'clock, and that nobody can come and pass the night with you."

The room held a bed with coarse sheets, two chairs, a little table, and a chest of drawers.

"How much will you board this young woman for?" said I.

He asked twenty sous, and two sous for the maid who would bring her meals and do her room.

"That will do," said the girl, and she paid the month's rent and the day's board. I left her telling her I would come back again.

As I went down the stairs I asked the old man to shew me a room for myself. He skewed me a very nice one at a Louis a month, and I paid in advance. He then gave me a latch-key, that I might go and come when I liked.

"If you wish to board here," said he, "I think I could give satisfaction."

Having done this good work, I had my dinner by myself, and then went to a coffee-house where I found the amiable Knight of Malta who was playing. He left the game as soon as he saw me, put the fistfull of gold he had won into his pocket, accosted me with the politeness natural to a Frenchman, and asked me how I had liked the lady who had given me my supper. I told him what had happened, at which he laughed, and asked me to come and see his ballet-girl. We found her under the hairdresser's hands, and she received me with the playful familiarity with which one greets an old acquaintance. I did not think much of her, but I pretended to be immensely struck, with the idea of pleasing the good-natured knight.

When the hairdresser left her, it was time for her to get ready for the theatre, and she dressed herself, without caring who was present. The knight helped her to change her chemise, which she allowed him to do as a matter of course, though indeed she begged me to excuse her.

As I owed her a compliment, I could think of nothing better than to tell her that though she had not offended me she had made me feel very uncomfortable.

"I don't believe you," said she.

"It's true all the same."

She came up to me to verify the fact, and finding I had deceived her, she said half crossly,

"You are a bad fellow."

The women of Marseilles are undoubtedly the most profligate in France. They not only pride themselves on never refusing, but also on being the first to propose. This girl skewed me a repeater, for which she had got up a lottery at twelve francs a ticket. She had ten tickets left; I took them all, and so delighted was she to touch my five Louis that she came and kissed me, and told the knight that her unfaithfulness to him rested only with me.

"I am charmed to hear it," said the Maltese. He asked me to sup with her, and I accepted the invitation, but the sole pleasure I had was looking at the knight at work. He was far inferior to Dolci!

I wished them good night, and went to the house where I had placed the poor girl. The maid skewed me to my room, and I asked her if I might go to the garret. She took the light, I followed her up, and Rosalie, as the poor girl was named, heard my voice and opened the door. I told the maid to wait for me in my room, and I went in and sat down on the bed.

"Are you contented, dear?" I said.

"I am quite happy."

"Then I hope you will be kind, and find room for me in your bed."

"You may come if you like, but I must tell you that you will not find me a maid, as I have had one lover."

"You told me a lie, then?"

"Forgive me, I could not guess you would be my lover."

"I forgive you willingly; all the more so as I am no great stickler for maidenheads."

She was as gentle as a lamb, and allowed me to gaze on all those charms of which my hands and my lips disputed the possession; and the notion that I was master of all these treasures put fire in all my veins, but her submissive air distressed me.

"How is it you do not partake my desires?" said I.

"I dare not, lest you take me for a pretender."

Artifice or studied coquetry might have prompted such an answer, but the real timidity and the frankness with which these words were uttered could not have been assumed. Impatient to gain possession of her I took off my clothes, and on getting into bed to her I was astonished to find her a maid.

"Why did you tell me you had a lover?" said I. "I never heard of a girl telling a lie of that sort before."

"All the same I did not tell a lie, but I am very glad that I seem as if
I had done so."

"Tell me all about it."

"Certainly I will, for I want to win your confidence. This is the story:

"Two years ago my mother, though she was hot-tempered, still loved me. I was a needle-woman, and earned from twenty to thirty sous a day. Whatever I earned I gave my mother. I had never had a lover, never thought of such a thing, and when my goodness was praised I felt inclined to laugh. I had been brought up from a child never to look at young men when I met them in the street, and never to reply to them when they addressed any impudence to me.

"Two months ago a fine enough looking young man, a native of Genoa, and a merchant in a small way, came to my mother to get her to wash some very fine cotton stockings which the sea-water had stained. When he saw me he was very complimentary, but in an honest way. I liked him, and, no doubt seeing it, he came and came again every evening. My mother was always present at our interviews, and he looked at me and talked to me, but did not so much as ask to kiss my hand. My mother was very pleased to notice that the young man liked me, and often scolded me because I was not polite enough to him. In time he had to go to Genoa in a small ship which belonged to him, and which was laden with goods. He assured us that he would return again the next spring and declare his intentions. He said he hoped he should find me as good as ever, and still without any lover. This was enough; my mother looked upon him as my betrothed, and let us talk together at the door till midnight. When he went I would shut the door and lie down beside my mother, who was always asleep.

"Four or five days before his departure, he took my arm and got me to go with him to a place about fifty paces from the house to drink a glass of Muscat at a Greek's, who kept his tavern open all night. We were only away for half an hour, and then it was that he first kissed me. When I got home I found my mother awake, and told her all; it seemed so harmless to me.

"Next day, excited by the recollection of what had happened the night before, I went with him again, and love began to gain ground. We indulged in caresses which were no longer innocent, as we well knew. However, we forgave each other, as we had abstained from the chief liberty.

"The day after, my lover—as he had to journey in the night—took leave of my mother, and as soon as she was in bed I was not longer in granting what I desired as much as he. We went to the

Greek's, ate and drank, and our heated senses gained love's cause; we forgot our duty, and fancied our misdemeanour a triumph.

"Afterwards we fell asleep, and when we awoke we saw our fault in the clear, cold light of day. We parted sorrowful rather than rejoicing, and the reception my mother gave me was like that you witnessed this morning. I assured her that marriage would take away the shame of my sin, and with this she took up a stick and would have done for me, if I had not taken to my heels, more from instinct than from any idea of what I was doing.

"Once in the street I knew not where to turn, and taking refuge in a church I stayed there like one in a dream till noon. Think of my position. I was hungry, I had no refuge, nothing but the clothes I wore, nothing that would get me a morsel of bread. A woman accosted me in the street. I knew her and I also knew that she kept a servants' agency. I asked her forthwith if she could get me a place.

"'I had enquiries about a maid this morning,' said she, 'but it is for a gay woman, and you are pretty. You would have a good deal of difficulty in remaining virtuous.'

"'I can keep off the infection,' I answered, 'and in the position I am in
I cannot pick and choose.'

"She thereupon took me to the lady, who was delighted to see me, and still more delighted when I told her that I had never had anything to do with a man. I have repented of this lie bitterly enough, for in the week I spent at that profligate woman's house I have had to endure the most humiliating insults that an honest girl ever suffered. No sooner did the men who came to the house hear that I was a maid than they longed to slake their brutal lust upon me, offering me gold if I would submit to their caresses. I refused and was reviled, but that was not all. Five or six times every day I was obliged to remain a witness of the disgusting scenes enacted between my mistress and her customers, who, when I was compelled to light them about the house at night, overwhelmed me with insults, because I would not do them a disgusting service for a twelve-sous piece. I could not bear this sort of life much longer, and I was thinking of drowning myself. When you came you treated me so ignominiously that my resolve to die was strengthened, but you were so kind and polite as you went away that I fell in love with you directly, thinking that Providence must have sent you to snatch me away from the abyss. I thought your fine presence might calm my mother and persuade her to take me back till my lover came to marry me. I was undeceived, and I saw that she took me for a prostitute. Now, if you like, I am altogether yours, and I renounce my lover of whom I am no longer worthy. Take me as your maid, I will love you and you only; I will submit myself to you and do whatever you bid me."

Whether it were weakness or virtue on my part, this tale of woe and a mother's too great severity drew tears from my eyes, and when she saw my emotion she wept profusely, for her heart was in need of some relief.

"I think, my poor Rosalie, you have only one chemise."

"Alas! that is all."

"Comfort yourself, my dear; all your wants shall be supplied tomorrow, and in the evening you shall sup with me in my room on the second floor. I will take care of you."

"You pity me, then?"

"I fancy there is more love than pity in it."

"Would to God it were so!"

This "would to God," which came from the very depths of her soul, sent me away in a merry mood. The servant who had been waiting for me for two hours, and was looking rather glum, relaxed when she saw the colour of a crown which I gave her by way of atonement.

"Tell your master," said I, "that Rosalie will sup with me to-morrow; let us have a fasting dinner, but let it be a good one."

I returned to my inn quite in love with Rosalie, and I congratulated myself on having at last heard a true tale from a pretty mouth. She appeared to me so well disposed that her small failing seemed to make her shine the more. I resolved never to abandon her, and I did so in all sincerity; was I not in love?

After I had had my chocolate next morning I went out with a guide to the shops, where I got the necessary articles, paying a good but not an excessive price. Rosalie was only fifteen, but with her figure, her well-formed breasts, and her rounded arms, she would have been taken for twenty. Her shape was so imprinted on my brain that everything I got for her fitted as if she had been measured for it. This shopping took up all the morning, and in the afternoon the man took her a small trunk containing two dresses, chemises, petticoats, handkerchiefs, stockings, gloves, caps, a pair of slippers, a fan, a work-bag, and a mantle. I was pleased at giving her such a delightful surprise, and I longed for suppertime that I might enjoy the sight of her pleasure.

The Knight of Malta came to dine with me without ceremony, and I was charmed to see him. After we had dined he persuaded me to go to the theatre, as in consequence of the suspense of the subscription arrangements the boxes would be filled with all the quality in Marseilles.

"There will be no loose women in the amphitheatre," said he, "as everybody has to pay."

That decided me and I went. He presented me to a lady with an excellent connection, who asked me to come and see her. I excused myself on the plea that I was leaving so shortly. Nevertheless she was very useful to me on my second visit to Marseilles. Her name was Madame Audibert.

I did not wait for the play to end, but went where love called me. I had a delightful surprise when I saw Rosalie; I should not have known her. But I cannot resist the pleasure of recalling her picture as she stood before me then, despite the years that have rolled by since that happy moment.

Rosalie was an enticing-looking brunette, above the middle height. Her face was a perfect oval, and exquisitely proportioned.

Two fine black eyes shed a soft and ravishing light around. Her eyebrows were arched, and she had a wealth of hair, black and shining as ebony; her skin was while and lightly tinged with colour. On her chin was a dimple, and her slightest smile summoned into being two other dimples, one on each cheek. Her mouth was small, disclosing two rows of fairest orient pearls, and from her red lips flowed forth an indefinable sweetness. The lower lip projected ever so lightly, and seemed designed to hold a kiss. I have spoken of her arms, her breast, and her figure, which left nothing to be desired, but I must add to this catalogue of her charms, that her hand was exquisitely shaped, and that her foot was the smallest I have ever seen. As to her other beauties, I will content myself with saying that they were in harmony with those I have described.

To see her at her best, one had to see her smiling; and hitherto she had been sad or vexed—states of mind which detract from a woman's appearance. But now sadness was gone, and gratitude and pleasure had taken its place. I examined her closely, and felt proud, as I saw what a transformation I had effected; but I concealed my surprise, lest she should think I had formed an unfavourable impression of her. I proceeded, therefore, to tell her that I should expose myself to ridicule if I attempted to keep a beauty like herself for a servant.

"You shall be my mistress," I said, "and my servants shall respect you as if you were my wife."

At this Rosalie, as if I had given her another being, began to try and express her gratitude for what I had done. Her words, which passion made confused, increased my joy; here was no art nor deceit, but simple nature.

There was no mirror in her garret, so she had dressed by her sense of touch, and I could see that she was afraid to stand up and look at herself in the mirror in my room. I knew the weak spot in all women's hearts (which men are very wrong in considering as matter for reproach), and I encouraged her to admire herself, whereupon she could not restrain a smile of satisfaction.

"I think I must be in disguise," said she, "for I have never seen myself so decked out before."

She praised the tasteful simplicity of the dress I had chosen, but was vexed at the thought that her mother would still be displeased.

"Think no more of your mother, dearest one. You look like a lady of quality, and I shall be quite proud when the people at Genoa ask me if you are my daughter."

"At Genoa?"

"Yes, at Genoa. Why do you blush?"

"From surprise; perhaps I may see there one whom I have not yet forgotten."

"Would you like to stay here better?"

"No, no! Love me and be sure that I love you and for your own sake, not from any thought of my own interests."

"You are moved, my angel; let me wipe away your tears with kisses."

She fell into my arms, and she relieved the various feelings of which her heart was full by weeping for some time. I did not try to console her, for she had not grief; she wept as tender souls, and women, more especially, often will. We had a delicious supper to which I did honour for two, for she ate nothing. I asked her if she was so unfortunate as not to care for good food.

"I have as good an appetite as anyone," she replied, "and an excellent digestion. You shall see for yourself when I grow more accustomed to my sudden happiness."

"At least you can drink; this wine is admirable. If you prefer Greek muscat I will send for some. It will remind you of your lover."

"If you love me at all, I beg you will spare me that mortification."

"You shall have no more mortification from me, I promise you. It was only a joke, and I beg your pardon for it."

"As I look upon you I feel in despair at not having known you first."

"That feeling of yours, which wells forth from the depths of your open soul, is grand. You are beautiful and good, for you only yielded to the voice of love with the prospect of becoming his wife; and when I think what you are to me I am in despair at not being sure you love me. An evil genius whispers in my ear that you only bear with me because I had the happiness of helping you."

"Indeed, that is an evil genius. To be sure, if I had met you in the street I should not have fallen head over ears in love with you, like a wanton, but you would certainly have pleased me. I am sure I love you, and not for what you have done for me; for if I were rich and you were poor, I would do anything in the world for you. But I don't want it to be like that, for I had rather be your debtor than for you to be mine. These are my real feelings, and you can guess the rest."

We were still talking on the same subject when midnight struck, and my old landlord came and asked me if I were pleased.

"I must thank you," I replied, "I am delighted. Who cooked this delicious supper?"

"My daughter."

"She understands her craft; tell her I thought it excellent."

"Yes, sir, but it is dear."

"Not too dear for me. You shall be pleased with me as I with you, and take care to have as good a supper to-morrow evening, as I hope the lady will be well enough to do justice to the products of your daughter's culinary skill."

"Bed is a capital place to get an appetite. Ah! it is sixty years since I have had anything to do with that sort of thing. What are you laughing at, mademoiselle?"

"At the delight with which you must recollect it."

"You are right, it is a pleasant recollection; and thus I am always ready to forgive young folks the peccadilloes that love makes them commit."

"You are a wise old man," said I, "everyone should sympathise with the tenderest of all our mortal follies."

"If the old man is wise," said Rosalie, when he had left the room, "my mother must be very foolish."

"Would you like me to take you to the play to-morrow?"

"Pray do not. I will come if you like, but it will vex me very much. I don't want to walk out with you or to go to the theatre with you here. Good heavens! What would people say. No, neither at Marseilles; but elsewhere, anything you please and with all my heart."

"Very good, my dear, just as you please. But look at your room; no more garret for you; and in three days we will start."

"So soon?"

"Yes; tell me to-morrow what you require for the journey, for I don't want you to lack for anything, and if you leave it all to me I might forget something which would vex me."

"Well, I should like another cloak, a cloak with a lining, some boots, a night-cap, and a prayer-book."

"You know how to read, do you?"

"Certainly; and I can write fairly well."

"I am glad to hear it. Your asking me so freely for what you want is a true proof of your love; where confidence dwells not there is no love. I will not forget anything, but your feet are so small that I should advise you to get your boots yourself."

Our talk was so pleasant, and I experienced such delight in studying her disposition, that we did not go to bed till five o'clock. In the arms of love and sleep we spent seven delicious hours, and when we rose at noon we were fast lovers. She called me thou, talked of love and not of gratitude, and, grown more familiar with her new estate, laughed at her troubles. She kissed me at every opportunity, called me her darling boy, her joy, and as the present moment is the only real thing in this life, I enjoyed her love, I was pleased with her caresses, and put away all ideas of the dreadful future, which has only one certainty—death, 'ultima linea rerum'.

The second night was far sweeter than the first; she had made a good supper, and drunk well, though moderately; thus she was disposed to refine on her pleasure, and to deliver herself with greater ardour to all the voluptuous enjoyments which love inspires.

I gave her a pretty watch and a gold shuttle for her to amuse herself with.

"I wanted it," said she, "but I should never have dared to ask for it."

I told her that this fear of my displeasure made me doubt once more whether she really loved me. She threw herself into my arms, and promised that henceforth she would shew me the utmost confidence.

I was pleased to educate this young girl, and I felt that when her mind had been developed she would be perfect.

On the fourth day I warned her to hold herself in readiness to start at a moment's notice. I had said nothing about my plans to Costa or Le Duc, but Rosalie knew that I had two servants, and I told her that I should often make them talk on the journey for the sake of the laughter their folly would afford me.

"You, my dear," I had said to her, "must be very reserved with them, and not allow them to take the slightest liberty. Give them your orders as a mistress, but without pride, and you will be obeyed and respected. If they forget themselves in the slightest particular, tell me at once."

I started from the hotel of the "Treize Cantons" with four post-horses, Le Duc and Costa sitting on the coachman's seat. The guide, whom I had paid well for his services, took us to Rosalie's door. I got out of the carriage, and after thanking the kindly old landlord, who was sorry to lose so good a boarder, I made her get in, sat down beside her, and ordered the postillions to go to Toulon, as I wished to see that fine port before returning to Italy. We got to Toulon at five o'clock.

My Rosalie behaved herself at supper like the mistress of a house accustomed to the best society. I noticed that Le Duc as head man made Costa wait upon her, but I got over him by telling my sweetheart that he would have the honour of doing her hair, as he could do it as well as the best barber in Paris. He swallowed the golden pill, and gave in with a good grace, and said, with a profound bow, that he hoped to give madam satisfaction.

We went out next morning to see the port, and were shewn over the place by the commandant, whose acquaintance we made by a lucky chance. He offered his arm to Rosalie, and treated her with the consideration she deserved for her appearance and the good sense of her questions. The commandant accepted my invitation to dinner, at which Rosalie spoke to the point though not to excess, and received the polite compliments of our worthy guest with much grace. In the afternoon he took us over the arsenal, and after having him to dinner could not refuse his invitation to supper. There was no difficulty about Rosalie; the commandant introduced her immediately to his wife, his daughter, and his son. I was delighted to see that her manner with ladies even surpassed her manner with gentlemen. She was one of Nature's own ladies. The commandant's wife and daughter caressed her again and again, and she received their attentions with that modest sensibility which is the seal of a good education.

They asked me to dinner the next day, but I was satisfied with what I had seen, so I took leave, intending to start on the morrow.

When we got back to the inn I told her how pleased I was with her, and she threw her arms round my neck for joy.

"I am always afraid," said she, "of being asked who I am."

"You needn't be afraid, dearest; in France no gentleman or lady would think of asking such a question."

"But if they did, what ought I to do?"

"You should make use of an evasion."

"What's an evasion?"

"A way of escaping from a difficulty without satisfying impertinent curiosity."

"Give me an example."

"Well, if such a question were asked you, you might say, 'You had better ask this gentleman.'"

"I see, the question is avoided; but is not that impolite?"

"Yes; but not so impolite as to ask an embarrassing question."

"And what would you say if the question was passed on to you?"

"Well, my answer would vary in a ratio with the respect in which I held the questioner. I would not tell the truth, but I should say something. And I am glad to see you attentive to my lessons. Always ask questions, and you will always find me ready to answer, for I want to teach you. And now let us to bed; we have to start for Antibes at an early hour, and love will reward you for the pleasure you have given me to-day."

At Antibes I hired a felucca to take me to Genoa, and as I intended to return by the same route I had my carriage warehoused for a small monthly payment. We started early with a good wind, but the sea becoming rough, and Rosalie being mortally afraid, I had the felucca rowed into Villafranca, where I engaged a carriage to take me to Nice. The weather kept us back for three days, and I felt obliged to call on the commandant, an old officer named Peterson.

He gave me an excellent reception, and after the usual compliments had passed, said,—

"Do you know a Russian who calls himself Charles Ivanoff?"

"I saw him once at Grenoble."

"It is said that he has escaped from Siberia, and that he is the younger son of the Duke of Courland."

"So I have heard, but I know no proof of his claim to the title."

"He is at Genoa, where it is said a banker is to give him twenty thousand crowns. In spite of that, no one would give him a sou here, so I sent him to Genoa at my own expense, to rid the place of him."

I felt very glad that the Russian had gone away before my arrival. An officer named Ramini, who was staying at the same inn as myself, asked if I would mind taking charge of a packet which M. de St. Pierre, the Spanish consul, had to send to the Marquis Grimaldi, at Genoa. It was the nobleman I had just seen at Avignon, and I was pleased to execute the commission. The same officer asked me whether I had ever seen a certain Madame Stuard.

"She came here a fortnight ago with a man who calls himself her husband. The poor devils hadn't a penny, and she, a great beauty, enchanted everybody, but would give no one a smile or a word."

"I have both seen and know her," I answered. "I furnished her with the means to come here. How could she leave Nice without any money?"

"That's just what no one can understand. She went off in a carriage, and the landlord's bill was paid. I was interested in the woman. The Marquis Grimaldi told me that she had refused a hundred louis he offered her, and that a Venetian of his acquaintance had fared just as badly. Perhaps that is you?"

"It is, and I gave her some money despite my treatment."

M. Peterson came to see me, and was enchanted with Rosalie's amiable manner. This was another conquest for her, and I duly complimented her upon it.

Nice is a terribly dull place, and strangers are tormented by the midges, who prefer them to the inhabitants. However, I amused myself at a small bank at faro, which was held at a coffee-house, and at which Rosalie, whose play I directed, won a score of Piedmontese pistoles. She put her little earnings into a purse, and told me she liked to have some money of her own. I scolded her for not having told me so before, and reminded her of her promise.

"I don't really want it," said she, "it's only my thoughtlessness."

We soon made up our little quarrel.

In such ways did I make this girl my own, in the hope that for the remnant of my days she would be mine, and so I should not be forced to fly from one lady to another. But inexorable fate ordained it otherwise.

The weather grew fine again, and we got on board once more, and the next day arrived at Genoa, which I had never seen before. I put up at "St. Martin's Inn," and for decency's sake took two rooms, but they were adjoining one another. The following day I sent the packet to M. Grimaldi, and a little later I left my card at his palace.

My guide took me to a linen-draper's, and I bought some stuff for Rosalie, who was in want of linen. She was very pleased with it.

We were still at table when the Marquis Grimaldi was announced; he kissed me and thanked me for bringing the parcel. His next remark referred to Madame Stuard. I told him what had happened, and he laughed, saying that he was not quite sure what he would have done under the circumstances.

I saw him looking at Rosalie attentively, and I told him she was as good as she was beautiful.

"I want to find her a maid," I said, "a good seamstress, who could go out with her, and above all who could talk Italian to her, for I want her to learn the language that I may take her into society at Florence, Rome and Naples."

"Don't deprive Genoa of the pleasure of entertaining her," said the marquis. "I will introduce her under whatever name she pleases, and in my own house to begin with."

"She has good reasons for preserving her incognito here."

"Ah, I see!—Do you think of staying here long?"

"A month, or thereabouts, and our pleasures will be limited to seeing the town and its surroundings and going to the theatre. We shall also enjoy the pleasures of the table. I hope to eat champignons every day, they are better here than anywhere else."

"An excellent plan. I couldn't suggest a better. I am going to see what I can do in the way of getting you a maid, mademoiselle."

"You sir? How can I deserve such great kindness?"

"My interest in you is the greater, as I think you come from Marseilles."

Rosalie blushed. She was not aware that she lisped, and that this betrayed her. I extricated her from her confusion by telling the marquis his conjecture was well founded.

I asked him how I could get the Journal de Savans, the Mercure de France, and other papers of the same description. He promised to send me a man who would get me all that kind of thing. He added that if I would allow him to send me some of his excellent chocolate he would come and breakfast with us. I said that both gift and guest were vastly agreeable to me.

As soon as he had gone Rosalie asked me to take her to a milliner's.

"I want ribbons and other little things," said she, "but I should like to bargain for them and pay for them out of my own money, without your having anything to do with it."

"Do whatever you like, my dear, and afterwards we will go to the play."

The milliner to whom we went proved to be a Frenchwoman. It was a charming sight to see Rosalie shopping. She put on an important air, seemed to know all about it, ordered bonnets in the latest fashion, bargained, and contrived to spend five or six louis with great grandeur. As we left the shop I told her that I had been taken for her footman, and I meant to be revenged. So saying, I made her come into a jeweller's, where I bought her a necklace, earrings, and brooches in imitation diamonds, and without letting her say a word I paid the price and left the shop.

"You have bought me some beautiful things," said she, "but you are too lavish with your money; if you had bargained you might have saved four louis at least."

"Very likely, dearest, but I never was any hand at a bargain."

I took her to the play, but as she did not understand the language she got dreadfully tired, and asked me to take her home at the end of the first act, which I did very willingly. When we got in I found a box waiting for me from M. Grimaldi. It proved to contain twenty-four pounds of chocolate. Costa, who had boasted of his skill in making chocolate in the Spanish fashion, received orders to make us three cups in the morning.

At nine o'clock the marquis arrived with a tradesman, who sold me some beautiful oriental materials. I gave them to Rosalie to make two 'mezzaro' for herself. The 'mezzaro' is a kind of hooded cloak worn by the Genoese women, as the 'cendal' is worn at Venice, and the 'mantilla' at Madrid.

I thanked M. Grimaldi for the chocolate, which was excellent; Costa was quite proud of the praise the marquis gave him. Le Duc came in to announce a woman, whose name I did not know.

"It's the mother of the maid I have engaged," said M. Grimaldi.

She came in, and I saw before me a well-dressed woman, followed by a girl from twenty to twenty-four years old, who pleased me at the first glance. The mother thanked the marquis, and presented her daughter to Rosalie, enumerating her good qualities, and telling her that she would serve her well, and walk with her when she wished to go out.

"My daughter," she added, "speaks French, and you will find her a good, faithful, and obliging girl."

She ended by saying that her daughter had been in service lately with a lady, and that she would be obliged if she could have her meals by herself.

The girl was named Veronique. Rosalie told her that she was a good girl, and that the only way to be respected was to be respectable. Veronique kissed her hand, the mother went away, and Rosalie took the girl into her room to begin her work.

I did not forget to thank the marquis, for he had evidently chosen a maid more with a view to my likings than to those of my sweetheart. I told him that I should not fail to call on him, and he replied that he would be happy to see me at any hour, and that I should easily find him at his casino at St. Pierre d'Arena, where he often spent the night.

The End

www.ingramcontent.com/pod-product-compliance
Lightning Source LLC
Chambersburg PA
CBHW072322290526
45794CB00002B/724